Wise Guy

31 Success Secrets of King Solomon

By

Al Fike, M.Div

WISE GUY:
31 Success Secrets of King Solomon
By Al Fike, M. Div

Formerly titled:
THE ULTIMATE SELF-HELP BOOK:
31 DAYS IN PROVERBS

2019-REVISED AND UPDATED
FOR AMAZON KINDLE AND OTHER DIGITAL READER
FORMATS

WISE GUY: 31 Success Secrets of King Solomon

ISBN-13: 978-1492277415
ISBN-10: 149227741X
Electronic version published by:
Al Fike Ministries, Inc
www.alfike.com
Print version published by:
CreateSpace.com, an Amazon Company
Printed in the United States of America
International copies are printed from other locations

Dedication

To my Daddy and Mama
(Johnnie and Norma Fike)

*Who taught us that following the Lord was the
wisest decision we could ever make.
Boy, were they ever right!*

What others say...

"Al effectively adds his personal touch to make Proverbs come to life."
—Zig Ziglar, Author,
See You at the Top

"Al's wonderful book will help you become a great success in your personal and business life."
—Truett Cathy, Chick-fil-A Founder,
Author, Eat More Chicken; Inspire More People

"This has practical, powerful and personal wisdom that will have a profound impact upon your life and relationships."
—Josh McDowell, Author,
More Than a Carpenter

"This book will help you to accomplish every dream God has inspired you to achieve!"
—Gary Smalley, Author
The DNA of Relationships

"It's like a compass, leading you step-by-step out of the forest and onto the highway of better living."
—Jim Rohn, Business Philosopher, *Author* Success Strategies

"This is a wonderful, uplifting, inspirational book, full of ideas and insights for better living."
**—Brian Tracy, *Author*
Psychology of Achievement**

"Gary Smalley first challenged me in 1974, to begin reading the Book of Proverbs every day. With Al Fike's wonderful new book, you will gain wisdom and insights that will change your life and the lives of those you love.
**—Steven K. Scott, *Author*
Mentored by a Millionaire**

"Al's unique book, "Wise Guy," will help you in each category of your life. His inspirational thoughts and lessons will provide you with plenty of strategies to tackle any challenge you're facing, and how to let God be in charge of all of it."
**—David Alvey, *President*
Aardvark Studios, Dallas, TX**

Table of Contents

Preface

We hear a lot about success and "self-help" these days. King Solomon believed in it, but just not in the way you might think. He understood that the best and most effective way to help himself was *not* to "help himself," but trust in someone much greater than he—the living God, his Creator! Solomon—by dedicating himself to the King of Kings—became the wisest human who ever lived on this earth (apart from Jesus Christ). I like to think of him as a true "Wise Guy" and a successful king, at least for most of his life.

Although Solomon was a wise man, and trusted God in his early life and middle-aged years, he certainly wasn't flawless. It was very unfortunate that he turned his back on God and His teachings later in his life by compromising with evil, and this got him into deep trouble. Solomon didn't personally apply all the wisdom God gave him to his *own* life. I do believe, however, he came to his senses later on and realized all the years he'd wasted. I think that's why he wrote the book of Ecclesiastes, which I'll discuss.

But this is very important to understand: Solomon's bad choices *did not negate* the validity of the proverbs God gave him to share with the rest of the world. Wisdom is concrete, and doesn't change any more than gravity. Sure, Solomon dropped the ball and made some stupid decisions, but God still used him as a conduit—like electricity through a copper wire—to get His wisdom out to His people, and thankfully, for us to live by today. Aren't you glad God uses people in spite of their short-comings? He can do the same thing with you and me today.

Solomon certainly made some wonderful accomplishments that are extremely helpful to us. I'm referring to the three books in the Old Testament that are attributed to him:

- The Song of Songs in his *early* years
- The Book of Proverbs in his *middle* years (he authored most of it, but not all, as you'll see)
- The Book of Ecclesiastes in his *later* years

In writing Ecclesiastes, I believe Solomon finally realized—after straying from the Lord—that whatever this temporal world has to offer in the way of happiness and fulfillment is extremely futile and a total waste of time—much like straightening the chairs on the Titanic. There are *far more* important things to focus on—like where you'll spend eternity, instead of chasing temporal, selfish ambitions! It's like my friend, Zig Ziglar, used to say: "You're going to be dead a lot longer than you're alive!" In other words, we will spend more time "out there" in eternity than we will *here* on this planet. And as my Dad admonished me from time to time, "You might want to get your butt in gear." And we need to get *ours* in gear and start making plans for eternity—like maybe *right now!*

In essence, Ecclesiastes could be summed up this way: *If you look at this world from a human standpoint, everything is a dead-end street, vane and massively depressing. But if you view life through God's "lens" and perspective, you'll discover that nothing matters more than your relationship with God.*

This "temporal" attitude is exactly what dominates this world we live in. People are into "self-help" instead of "God-help," or more importantly, "God-*overhaul.*"

I have discovered that we help ourselves the most when we realize the futility of the current modern "self-help" mindset and latch on to God's wisdom and His way of thinking. I truly believe that God's way is best!

Much like opening the lid on a grand piano for the first time, God's wisdom will bring music to your soul like you've never known before. You'll begin to see how every key facet of your life will improve and become more meaningful as you allow the Lord to take control. I believe you'll never look back once you "help yourself" to Him!

In this book (which I pretty much wrote for myself), you'll find what I call "Secrets"—inspirational stories and lessons—of truth based on the Book of Proverbs. I hope you'll find guidance for your personal, family and career journeys.

In each chapter, the complete easy-to-read New Living Translation text from each chapter of Proverbs is included. And yes, my ultimate goal is to get you to *read* Proverbs, whether it's from *this* book, or *your own* Bible. I hope these lessons will add a little something extra that you can apply to your life. Here are a few treasures I believe you'll discover:

- How to make better decisions
- The power of setting and achieving goals
- How to replace bad habits with good ones
- The hidden keys to great relationships
- What true wisdom is, and how to obtain it
- How to experience happiness and fulfillment
- God's purpose and direction for your life
- What it means to live abundantly
- How to think the way God thinks
- ...plus much more!

A Brief Background of Proverbs

My goal in providing some history and background of Proverbs is NOT to bore you with a ton of details, but simply to give you a backdrop view so the rest of the book will come alive as you meditate on the chapters and verses.

It's critically important before reading any book of the Bible to gain some insight as to the purpose and reason for the book, etc. It's like what small tiles do for a mosaic. Each piece makes the picture come alive, especially when you back away and get a broader view.

Understanding the background helps solidify and illuminate the message and get a broader picture of the author's intent. I highly recommend reading the Tyndale Life Application Bible notes related to the introduction of Proverbs. I've shared some of it in the following, along with other sources.

It's obvious from the first phrase of Proverbs that King Solomon is clearly the author.

Solomon, as you may know, was the son of King David and Bathsheba, and ruled in Israel for forty years (970-930 B.C.). He was the one who built the great Jerusalem temple (1 Kings 6-8), and served as Israel's wise judge (1 Kings 3:16).

He brought Israel into international status through his marriage alliances (1 Kings 11), his amazing ability to answer difficult questions (1 Kings 10:1), and his prolific literary activity (1 Kings 4:32).

However, the debatable part has been his exact role in the final shaping of this collection of wisdom. We know that he was a collector of many proverbs and wise sayings, but the actual collection of the Book of Proverbs seems to have taken shape *after* Solomon's time, because we know that Hezekiah's scribes (715-686 B.C.) selected proverbs out of an older collection of Solomon's (see Proverbs 25:1).

While much of the material dates from the time of Solomon, it was not canonized (classified as holy, or sacred) until much later. The exact dates of Kings Lemuel and Agur and the Sayings of the Wise are unknown (see Proverbs 22:17; Proverbs 24:23).

According to several commentaries—primarily the Life Application Bible—there are a few points to keep in mind about the nature of proverbs. A proverb is a wise saying delivered in a poetic manner, considered strategically brief, well-crafted and true; and they're also based on principles, not conjecture or supposition.

1. **Proverbs are short and concise.** They are most often contained in a single sentence composed of two poetic lines (see Proverbs 10:1). It was well known that the wise spoke only a few well-chosen words and the audience was expected to search out, pursue, and develop their full meaning and apply it to their own lives (10:19; 17:28).

2. **Proverbs are well-crafted.** This is because they are a highly developed form of poetry. The poetic sense often comes alive by the use of rhetorical devices, especially **metaphor** (10:25), **simile** (10:26), and **synecdoche**, which is a figure of speech in which the word for part of something is used to mean the whole, for example, "sail" for "boat," or vice versa (10:21).

3. **Proverbs are solid or concrete.** They often are snapshots of common events. Some examples

would be the animal world (Proverbs 6:6; 23:5), family and friends (10:1; 12:4; 17:17), or society— from the king and his court (16:12) to his lowliest servant (14:35). Proverbs deals a lot with morality issues (see 10:4). Proverbs calls for us to search for, discover, and observe the patterns in every area of life. It teaches that fearing God is the most important principle of wisdom.

4. **Proverbs are not to be confused with promises.** While promises are statements that God guarantees, proverbs only state what generally happens much of the time. Proverbs do not necessarily guarantee that, in every case, the end result of an action will follow. For example, to say that diligence always leads to wealth (Proverbs 10:4), may not always be the case. In poverty-stricken areas where people work very hard, regardless of their diligence, they can still remain in poverty because of those conditions.

I think it's important to show you how the Book of Proverbs is divided. There are five general sections to the book.

1. **The Importance of Wisdom** (Proverbs 1-9). The young man addressed is advised to embrace Wisdom and to avoid the adulteress Folly.

2. **The Proverbial Sayings of Solomon, Part 1** (Proverbs 10:1-22:16). These contain short two-line proverbial sayings that probably came from Solomon.

3. **The Sayings of the Wise** (Proverbs 22:17-24:34). These sayings deal with concerns similar

to those addressed by proverbs found in Egypt.

4. **The Proverbial Sayings of Solomon, Part 2** (Proverbs 25-29). This section returns to the Solomonic proverbs, like those in Proverbs 10-22. These were probably edited by Hezekiah's men.

5. **The Wisdom from Foreign Kings** (Proverbs 30-31). This is a collection of wisdom from: the sayings of Agur (Proverbs 30:1-33) and the sayings of Lemuel (Proverbs 31:1-9), with the concluding lyrical segment describing the virtuous woman (Proverbs 31:10-31).

There is much more introductory information on the Book of Proverbs that you can research on your own. My purpose here is simply to give you a brief history and background so that you'll have a clearer understanding of the book and what God is trying to communicate through these wise sayings.

I'm convinced this book of wise instruction will change your life, just as it has mine. But real success is only experienced when we *apply* the truth of what God is trying to teach us. Meditating on these proverbs daily has great benefits: we will live more wisely, stay out of trouble, and be a lot happier. This is my wish for you.

Introduction

During my senior year in high school, I had a lot of fun dabbling in photography. This skill came in pretty handy, because I had just entered the ministry as a traveling speaker and needed some publicity photos.

One afternoon, my friend, John Turner, who owned our local newspaper, let me use his photo dark room. Back in those days, photo development involved a tedious, manual process (not like it is in our digital age today) that required a few steps.

After developing the negatives and making imprints on the photo paper, the pictures had to be soaked in chemicals, rinsed, and then hung up to dry. Once the sheets dried, they would curl upwards. Noticing this, John gave me some good advice I'd never really thought about. He said, "Al, if you'll put those pictures in a book, it'll straighten them out."

Sometime later, for some reason, what John said popped up in my mind. Then all of a sudden, *WHAM*, it hit me, like one of David's stones in Goliath's forehead. It was like God said to me, *"Al, if you will put your life in my book (the Bible), you'll stay straight."*

Back then, I read the Bible occasionally, but after this revelation, I began reading it on a regular basis. Somehow—I'm sure by God's direction—I happened upon and fell in love with the Book of Proverbs. I felt like I had been lost in a forest and, all of sudden, stumbled upon a compass! His Word became SO valuable to me. I experienced a heart-change and gained insights into God's wisdom, guidance and purpose for my life that I had never known before.

When I was a young kid, I liked playing in the yard with magnifying glasses (most boys did). Holding it over a leaf, I would line it up with the sun and harness its rays to create my own little "laser beam," and I'd burn a hole right through that leaf! (I also experimented on a few ants and other bugs, and it was NOT a fragrant aroma!)

The Book of Proverbs (along with the rest of the Bible) became like that magnifying glass—igniting a fire deep in my soul. I developed a yearning to live and conduct myself the way God wanted me to, and my relationship with Him grew like never before.

I discovered that I could no longer just *read* His words, and not make an attempt to *do* anything about them—that is, to obey God. And, strangely enough, I did all this because I *wanted* to. I was falling more and more in love with God, and obeying Him because of my love for Him. (It was never because I was afraid of what He'd *do to me* if I didn't). And this is what a love relationship is supposed to be anyway.

To boil it all down, as I continued exploring Proverbs, I felt like God was working in my life in three distinct ways:

- He was giving me direction and purpose
- He was correcting my thinking
- He was increasing my desire to serve Him

Webster's definition of "proverb" is a "wise saying." But while working on this book I took the liberty to develop my own "definition."

Dividing the word "proverb," I came up with "pro" (meaning "for") and "verb" (meaning "action"). I thought to myself, *That's it! "Proverb" is Pro-Verb—for action! I'm supposed to do the stuff God says!* It reminds me of what James, the brother of Jesus, writes when he says, "But don't just listen to God's word. You must do what it says. Otherwise, you are only fooling yourselves" (James 1:22). I had been fooling myself long enough, and I was tired of playing that game.

After reading dozens of self-help books over the years, I realized *I* needed help—help from above—because I was worn out trying to do something I was never designed to do—taking control of my own life.

Here's one treasure I discovered: Everything I need to be successful in every aspect of my life is already found in Solomon's 31-chapter book!

Proverbs, along with the rest of the Bible, is about trusting in God, listening to Him and taking ownership and responsibility for how we think about God, others, ourselves, and our circumstances. Like it or not, we can't always control what happens *to* us, but we are responsible for our *responses* and *reactions* to those situations. That applies to our attitude, career, family, health, marriage, time, goals, education, and decisions. And here's the big one: we are accountable and responsible for our response to the Lord's invitation to personally follow Him.

You may be asking, *"How am I responsible for my relationship with God?"* Let me illustrate.

Many years ago I was shopping for a new car (actually it was pre-owned, but new to me). A flyer was posted on one of the car windows, showing the driver buckling his seat belt. At the bottom was the caption: "We've done our part; you do yours." The manufacturer provided the seat belt, now it's up to me, the driver, to buckle up! *I* am responsible for the *clicking* part! If I wreck the car and become injured, I can't blame the car dealer or the manufacturer for my negligence and stupidity for refusing to put on my seatbelt!

God has already done His part by giving us His Word, His instruction book (the Bible) on how to live, conduct ourselves and get the most out of life. It's up to *us* to *listen* to Him and *follow* what He says.

The most important thing God has done for us is giving us His Son, Jesus Christ, to die on the cross for our sins, for which we deserve the full punishment. As a result of His goodness and mercy, all we have to do is *trust* Him for what He's done (and finished) through Christ's dying and coming back to life on our behalf. We "buckle up" when we trust Him and turn our lives over to Him as Lord and Savior. That is *our* responsibility!

The word "responsibility" means "response-ability"—the "ability to respond." It means that we decide to *own* (or, own up to) what happens in our lives. We stop blaming others or circumstances when situations aren't in our favor. When we *respond* properly (rather than *react*; reacting is more negative), we set ourselves up to make different choices that lead to better outcomes. But these positive outcomes will be impossible while we're playing the "blame game." I know people who have "blame lists" a mile high.

One of my favorite teachers was the late Jim Rohn. (I have every one of his audio recordings, and they are wonderful!) Jim tells a story about his blame list. One day, when his boss and mentor, Mr. Earl Shoaff, reviewed his list, he simply looked at it and said, "Jim, there's only one problem with your list." And Jim asked, "What's that?" He responded, "*You* ain't on it!"

What about you? Are you on *your* blame list? And is *your* name at the top? Your road to success in life begins with this admission.

Proverbs is about taking charge—not *you*, but allowing GOD to be the Commander and Chief of your life. It's about *your* choosing to be responsible by accepting and obeying Him.

As we think about Solomon's teachings, I want you to notice how responsibility fits into each one of the items listed below. These subjects and more are discussed in Proverbs:

- How to make better decisions and choices
- How to get along with others
- How to raise your children
- How to manage your finances

- How to form good habits
- How to find hope
- How to stay out of trouble
- How to overcome fear
- How to be a real winner
- How to be courageous
- How to achieve your dreams
- How to find the right mate
- How to succeed in business
- How to have a relationship with God

Taking responsibility can be difficult and uncomfortable at times, but it certainly has its rewards.

If you've ever climbed to the top of a mountain, you know the excitement of finally reaching the top, right? Check out these benefits:

1. The view is better
2. The air is fresher
3. The crowd is smaller
4. There's *more light*!

Number four is my favorite.

But how is there more light? Think about it. When the sun rises, the apex is the first place the light hits and, by evening, it's the last place the sun touches. You enjoy more light when you're on the top!

Listening to God and following His wisdom is a lot like hanging out on that peak. I believe this is where God wants us to be, or at least moving in that direction.

One of my favorite passages summarizes the entire Book of Proverbs: "Trust in the Lord with all your heart and do not depend on your own understanding; seek His will in all you do, and He will show you which path to take" (Proverbs 3:5-6). That's a great promise, as well as a wonderful partnership—with God! But remember, *we* are responsible for the path we choose.

The Book of Proverbs teaches us how to live wisely. And the great news is that we don't have to do it by ourselves! God (through His Holy Spirit) is in us as believers in Christ, helping us to follow and obey Him. HE is our strength!

Patrick Overton describes very well how God is always close to us:

When you come to the edge of all the light you have, and you take that step into the darkness of the unknown;

You must believe that one of two things will happen: either there will be something solid for you to stand on, or else, God will teach you how to fly.

"Rebuilding the Front Porch of America"
Copyright Patrick Overton, 1997

I hope you are richly blessed by these daily lessons and devotions in Proverbs. Maybe just one little phrase or nugget could encourage and change your life on any given day. So here's my desire for you: *I pray that the compound interest of God's wisdom brings you so many rewards in life, that by Day 31, the amount of wealth you receive could never be measured in currency!* – Al Fike

– Secret 1 –
Let Loose

*There is only one way to put an end to evil, and
that is to do good for evil.*
– Leo Tolstoy

There's an old fable about an Indian who was out hunting one beautiful afternoon.

Sitting on a rock to take a short break, he noticed a beautiful bald eagle soaring high in the sky. He was captivated by its majesty and strength.

But all of a sudden, he noticed that the eagle appeared to spot "dinner" moving below and then swooped down for the attack. Momentarily, the Indian lost sight of the bird, but soon, he gained altitude once again—clutching his prey in the tight grip of his talons.

Continuing to gaze at the bird, something strange began to happen. The eagle seemed to struggle. A few moments later, he faltered, and faltered even more, and finally plummeted to the rocky ground below.

After searching for more than an hour, the curious Indian eventually found him. The enormous bird was lying face down, his wings spread—and still hanging on to his catch. But what caused his rapid descent? That "little" animal he was clinging to just happen to be a badger—known for their viciousness and razor-sharp teeth. During the struggle, the desperate badger— fighting for his life—began taking bites from the eagle's breast, leaving the bird mortally wounded. And it was all because of one simple reason: the eagle wouldn't let go! Not *could not*; *would not*!

Foolish choices always come with a high price tag, don't they?

Sometimes, acting no differently than that eagle, we humans tend to do the same thing. We covet something that could be very destructive, and then proceed with little thought, not realizing there will be consequences looming just ahead for that unwise choice. Deep down we know it's not the best "catch" to pursue, and even after latching on, we know we should let go, yet we are reluctant and hang on anyway; then follows the crash.

I wish I could open everyone's head and pour in this simple truth: God's love for us is so immense and beyond our comprehension. He wants what's best for us and wants us to "let go of sin"—not because of what *He* will do to us, but because of what *sin* does to us. This is the reason He hates sin so much—He sees what it does to His kids.

If you have never decided to become a follower of Jesus Christ, you should! Why? Because God *wants* you! The Bible says that He *loves* you and wants to have a personal relationship and connection with *you*. He wants you to follow Him because *He* is the way to everlasting life!

The only thing God does not love is *sin*! He's doesn't hate *you*, but He hates your sin and rebellion. He does not—I repeat, does not—want you to perish and spend eternity without Him (John 3:16). But if you hang on to your rebellion, and reject His offer for the forgiveness of your sin, the only outcome is eternal devastation. If you say, "That's not fair," well, yes it is! God didn't screw up; *you and I did*. He's perfect and holy, we're not! God is on the winning side; without Him, we're on the losing side. I invite you to come on over to His team! You will *not* be sorry, I promise.

God not only verbally tells us that He loves us, but He actually *demonstrated* that great love. He paid our sin debt; and because of that payment, we have the wonderful privilege to claim the *free gift* of eternal life. We don't have to work for it, or pay Him for the gift. All we have to do is believe in Him and accept Him into our lives. You might ask, "Is that all there is too it?" Yep, that's it; it truly is just *that* simple!

Once you become a follower of Christ, God doesn't leave you "in the dark." He provides His Word, the Bible, as your instruction guide on how to live and how to please Him. His presence and guidance, in turn, will also make you happy and fulfilled. There will be a peace like you've never known before.

Once you decide to trust Him, now the journey of abundant living begins. We have the whole Bible, including this great book of Proverbs, to show us and teach us about God's wisdom, ways and mindset. His Word instructs us on how to pursue what is right and pure, and how to let go of what is sinful and harmful. Wisdom warns: "For...their own complacency will destroy them. But all who listen to me will live in peace and safety, unafraid of harm" (Proverbs 1:32-33). Everyone wants freedom, peace and safety, right? When we walk with God, we can have all of these. We'll be able to "fly" to new heights, as well as experience true freedom without crashing and destroying our lives.

In this first chapter, Solomon gives us an overall view of the nature of Proverbs, and this basically sets the tone for the rest of this great book.

Let me encourage you to take your time and try not to rush through any of these chapters. Make the effort to absorb the rich content of each verse, as much as you can. This book is so rich with tools for happy living.

As you read and reflect on today's chapter, keep an eye out for the verses that admonish you to relinquish what is bad and treasure what is good. Then ask yourself the question: *What is it in my life that needs to be released in order to pursue the best—GOD'S best?*

Do yourself a favor—let it go!

Proverbs 1

1 These are the proverbs of Solomon, David's son, king of Israel.

2 The purpose of these proverbs is to teach people wisdom and discipline, and to help them understand wise sayings.

3 Through these proverbs, people will receive instruction in discipline, good conduct, and doing what is right, just, and fair.

4 These proverbs will make the simpleminded clever. They will give knowledge and purpose to young people.

5 Let those who are wise listen to these proverbs and become even wiser. And let those who understand receive guidance

6 by exploring the depth of meaning in these proverbs, parables, wise sayings, and riddles.

7 Fear of the Lord is the beginning of knowledge. Only fools despise wisdom and discipline.

8 Listen, my child, to what your father teaches you. Don't neglect your mother's teaching.

9 What you learn from them will crown you with grace and clothe you with honor.

10 My child, if sinners entice you, turn your back on them!

11 They may say, "Come and join us. Let's hide and kill someone! Let's ambush the innocent!

12 Let's swallow them alive as the grave swallows its victims. Though they are in the prime of life, they will go down into the pit of death.

13 And the loot we'll get! We'll fill our houses with all kinds of things!

14 Come on, throw in your lot with us; we'll split our loot with you."

15 Don't go along with them, my child! Stay far away from their paths.

16 They rush to commit crimes. They hurry to commit murder.

17 When a bird sees a trap being set, it stays away.

18 But not these people! They set an ambush for themselves; they booby-trap their own lives!

19 Such is the fate of all who are greedy for gain. It ends up robbing them of life.

20 Wisdom shouts in the streets. She cries out in the public square.

21 She calls out to the crowds along the main street, and to those in front of city hall.

22 "You simpletons!" she cries. "How long will you go on being simpleminded? How long will you mockers relish your mocking? How long will you fools fight the facts?

23 Come here and listen to me! I'll pour out the spirit of wisdom upon you and make you wise.

24 "I called you so often, but you didn't come. I reached out to you, but you paid no attention.

25 You ignored my advice and rejected the correction I offered.

26 So I will laugh when you are in trouble! I will mock you when disaster overtakes you—

27 when calamity overcomes you like a storm, when you are engulfed by trouble, and when anguish and distress overwhelm you.

28 "I will not answer when they cry for help. Even though they anxiously search for me, they will not find me.

29 For they hated knowledge and chose not to fear the Lord.

30 They rejected my advice and paid no attention when I corrected them.

31 That is why they must eat the bitter fruit of living their own way. They must experience the full terror of the path they have chosen.

32 For they are simpletons who turn away from me—to death. They are fools, and their own complacency will destroy them.

33 But all who listen to me will live in peace and safety, unafraid of harm."

Questions for Reflection

1. What are you hanging on to that needs to be handed over to God?

2. Why do many people think that God is punishing them?

3. What is the difference between punishment and discipline?

4. Who usually gets blamed when things go wrong?

5. What does it mean to "take responsibility?"

Prayer:

Lord, You know what's going on in my life. I also know that You know what's best for me, even when I don't "feel" it. Help me to let go of everything that is harmful to me and hang on to what pleases You.

– Secret 2 –
Daydream Daily

Vision is the art of seeing things invisible.
– Jonathan Swift

Recently, I heard a story about an elementary school teacher who was giving her students a homework assignment, when she noticed one little girl, Emma, gazing out the window, somewhat mesmerized.

Annoyed by this, the teacher, Mrs. Jackson, abruptly stopped talking, and in a few seconds the entire class was staring at this unsuspecting "day dreamer."

Finally Emma, realizing things were much too quiet—except for an occasional snicker from one of the students—turned to face Mrs. Jackson.

"What are you doing?" chastised the teacher.

"I was thinking," the startled Emma replied.

"Well, don't you know you're not supposed to think in school?" commented Mrs. Jackson. After a moment of stunned silence, the children burst into laughter, totally embarrassing the teacher.

The late, great co-founder of the Nightingale-Conant Corporation, Earl Nightingale, reminds us: "When young minds are churning, actively thinking, they are performing the highest function of humanity. Indulging in daydreaming is not necessarily a waste of time. Often it is quite the opposite, especially when our focus is on a particular goal or project. This mental process has led to many of the benefits we enjoy today— modern conveniences, scientific breakthroughs, books and motion pictures."

As you read Proverbs 2 today, you'll see the correlation between knowledge and wisdom. Instruction is important, but it is critical that you use your God-given creativity to "connect the dots" and make that teaching relevant to your situation.

King Solomon writes: "Cry out for insight and understanding. Search for them as you would for lost money or hidden treasure" (Proverbs 2:3-4).

Do you realize that we have only scratched the surface of our God-given creativity and potential? When our imagination is allowed to "fly out the window," there's no telling what great works God can accomplish through us, especially when we are staying connected with Him in prayer and meditating upon His Word (see Joshua 1).

I once heard about a cartoon showing a class of prehistoric children being taught how to hunt deer. The cave man teacher turns to scold a little boy and reprimand him for whittling on a piece of wood.

He asks, "Don't you want to keep up with the other children?" The next scene shows the "cave kid" whittling an airplane! I think it's interesting how the cartoonist depicted just how far back creative thinking goes. Of course, we know that it really goes back to the creation of man and woman.

Since God created our minds, I believe that, when we allow Him to guide our thinking and spark the creative fire in our minds, as Solomon says, "you will know how to find the right course of action every time" (Proverbs 2:9).

Here's something I've thought about and believe to be true: "Effective daydreaming can prevent nightmares." Why do I believe this? Because when our minds are focused on a dream or goal we eagerly want to achieve, we don't have time to worry about all the bad stuff that's going on around us. We begin dreaming about our dreams, instead of fantasizing about our worries.

Become a creative, productive daydreamer. But don't just dream; *act* on your ideas! The sky can be the limit on what God can accomplish through us, if we let Him!

Proverbs 2

1 My child, listen to me and treasure my instructions.

2 Tune your ears to wisdom, and concentrate on understanding.

3 Cry out for insight and understanding.

4 Search for them as you would for lost money or hidden treasure.

5 Then you will understand what it means to fear the Lord, and you will gain knowledge of God.

6 For the Lord grants wisdom! From his mouth come knowledge and understanding.

7 He grants a treasure of good sense to the godly. He is their shield, protecting those who walk with integrity.

8 He guards the paths of justice and protects those who are faithful to him.

9 Then you will understand what is right, just, and fair, and you will know how to find the right course of action every time.

10 For wisdom will enter your heart, and knowledge will fill you with joy.

11 Wise planning will watch over you. Understanding will keep you safe.

12 Wisdom will save you from evil people, from those whose speech is corrupt.

13 These people turn from right ways to walk down dark and evil paths.

14 They rejoice in doing wrong, and they enjoy evil as it turns things upside down.

15 What they do is crooked, and their ways are wrong.

16 Wisdom will save you from the immoral woman, from the flattery of the adulterous woman.

17 She has abandoned her husband and ignores the covenant she made before God.

18 Entering her house leads to death; it is the road to hell.

19 The man who visits her is doomed. He will never reach the paths of life.

20 Follow the steps of good men instead, and stay on the paths of the righteous.

21 For only the upright will live in the land, and those who have integrity will remain in it.

22 But the wicked will be removed from the land, and the treacherous will be destroyed.

Questions for Reflection:

1. When you daydream, what do you mostly think about? Is God first and foremost in your thoughts?

2. When was the last time you found a quiet place and did some daydream-type thinking?

3. In your hectic schedule, how can you set aside time for brainstorming and creative thinking?

4. In what areas of your life should you more passionately seek God's wisdom and His way of thinking?

Prayer:

Lord, I give my mind and my thoughts to You. Fill me with Your knowledge, understanding and great wisdom. Help me to see my life and situations from Your perspective.

– Secret 3 –
Practice Presence

Concentrate all your thoughts upon the work at hand. The sun's rays do not burn until brought to a focus.
– Alexander Graham Bell

Several years ago, a ten-year-old girl named Patti attended a school assembly program with about 300 other students in Atlanta, Georgia. A registered nurse was the guest speaker and gave a presentation on how to save someone by performing CPR. Patti listened attentively to the instructor—glued to every word.

However, many of her peers were bored, whispering and giggling with each other, making it hard for Patti to concentrate, but she listened anyway.

The assembly program concluded, and Patti went about her school day—and eventually her childhood. She never dreamed some twenty-two years later that brief thirty-minute instruction would become so pivotal—after her three-year-old nephew fell into her swimming pool in Florida and nearly drowned. The "long-ago" information she had absorbed and filed away instantly came back to her—all because she *paid attention*! She was very much "in the present moment." She was *there*! Let me also add that I'm especially grateful she listened, because if she hadn't, our son, Skyler, would not be alive today.

In our fast-paced culture, we are constantly bombarded with a steady stream of data along with massive amounts of distractions. And who knows when an idea—or solution to a perplexing problem—will suddenly surface, like a cork from the bottom of a bucket of water?

And what if that idea was one that could dramatically change your life or someone else's for the better? You wouldn't want to miss out on *that* opportunity, would you? In the words of the late business philosopher, Jim Rohn: "Wherever you are, *be there!*"

Proverbs teaches us this: "My child, never forget the things I have taught you. Store my commands in your heart, for they will give you a long and satisfying life" (Proverbs 3:1-2). In other words, remember it and store it!

The older I get, it becomes much easier to let things slip by me. Paying attention has always been a challenge, and I really have to work at it. If I don't keep a "to do" list, I'm pretty much done for. A friend of mine once told me, "Feeling listless? Make a list." A list helps me stay on target with my days. I couldn't function with out it.

Did you know that throughout the Bible, the Lord repeatedly tells us to be aware and alert, to pay attention? Here are just three instances:

1. In Ezekiel's vision of God, the prophet was told: "Pay close attention to everything I show you" (Ezekiel 40:4).

2. Jesus said: "...be sure to pay attention to what you hear. To those who are open to my teaching, more understanding will be given" (Luke 8:18).

3. God's Word warns us "we must listen very carefully to the truth we have heard, or we may drift away from it" (Hebrews 2:1).

If paying attention and listening were not important, God would not have mentioned it in the Bible. The reason why God tells us to *remember* is because we keep *forgetting!*

Have you noticed that there's a cost involved with paying attention. That's why the word *pay* is in that phrase. It costs something to *pay attention*, to be "in the moment." We have to put in some effort and discipline.

Who knows what today holds that will demand our undivided attention. Let's do whatever it takes to get ourselves back into reality, where we are right now. Then good things just might begin unfolding for us—such as saving someone's life!

Take it from Patti—practice *being there*!

Proverbs 3

1 My child, never forget the things I have taught you. Store my commands in your heart,

2 for they will give you a long and satisfying life.

3 Never let loyalty and kindness get away from you! Wear them like a necklace; write them deep within your heart.

4 Then you will find favor with both God and people, and you will gain a good reputation.

5 Trust in the Lord with all your heart; do not depend on your own understanding.

6 Seek his will in all you do, and he will direct your paths.

7 Don't be impressed with your own wisdom. Instead, fear the Lord and turn your back on evil.

8 Then you will gain renewed health and vitality.

9 Honor the Lord with your wealth and with the best part of everything your land produces.

10 Then he will fill your barns with grain, and your vats will overflow with the finest wine.

11 My child, don't ignore it when the Lord disciplines you, and don't be discouraged when he corrects you.

12 For the Lord corrects those he loves, just as a father corrects a child in whom he delights.

13 Happy is the person who finds wisdom and gains understanding.

14 For the profit of wisdom is better than silver, and her wages are better than gold.

15 Wisdom is more precious than rubies; nothing you desire can compare with her.

16 She offers you life in her right hand, and riches and honor in her left.

17 She will guide you down delightful paths; all her ways are satisfying.

18 Wisdom is a tree of life to those who embrace her; happy are those who hold her tightly.

19 By wisdom the Lord founded the earth; by understanding he established the heavens.

20 By his knowledge the deep fountains of the earth burst forth, and the clouds poured down rain.

21 My child, don't lose sight of good planning and insight. Hang on to them,

22 for they fill you with life and bring you honor and respect.

23 They keep you safe on your way and keep your feet from stumbling.

24 You can lie down without fear and enjoy pleasant dreams.

25 You need not be afraid of disaster or the destruction that comes upon the wicked,

26 for the Lord is your security. He will keep your foot from being caught in a trap.

27 Do not withhold good from those who deserve it when it's in your power to help them.

28 If you can help your neighbor now, don't say, "Come back tomorrow, and then I'll help you."

29 Do not plot against your neighbors, for they trust you.

30 Don't make accusations against someone who hasn't wronged you.

31 Do not envy violent people; don't copy their ways.

32 Such wicked people are an abomination to the Lord, but he offers his friendship to the godly.

33 The curse of the Lord is on the house of the wicked, but his blessing is on the home of the upright.

34 The Lord mocks at mockers, but he shows favor to the humble.

35 The wise inherit honor, but fools are put to shame!

Questions for Reflection:

1. What interrupts your ability to focus and concentrate? How can that be improved?

2. How can you prevent "wrong thoughts" from dominating your thinking?

3. What steps can you take to make certain God's Word becomes your main focus on a daily basis?

Prayer:

Father, please turn my attention to those things that are truly important, and that really make a difference. Your Word teaches me Your desire and will for my life. Help me to focus all my attention on what you tell me in your Word.

– Secret 4 –
Persevere Passionately

By perseverance, the snail reached the ark.
– Charles H. Spurgeon

Christopher Reeve said, "A hero is an ordinary individual who finds the strength to persevere and endure in spite of overwhelming obstacles." And he most certainly was speaking firsthand about it.

The difference between eminently successful people and "also-rans" is found in one word: perseverance. Those who triumph don't settle for second best, or failure. They experience it, but they simply keep moving forward. And they do it with passion.

Here are just a few inspiring examples of passionate perseverance:

1. Albert Einstein's Ph.D. dissertation was rejected by the University of Bern, in Switzerland. They said it was "irrelevant and fanciful."

2. Abraham Lincoln lost eight elections and failed miserably in business before realizing his dream to become the President of the United States.

3. Thomas Edison unsuccessfully attempted to create an incandescent lamp—not once, but thousands of times—before his light bulb worked.

4. Henry Ford faced bankruptcy three times before succeeding to mass produce automobiles.

5. Nineteenth century novelist, John Creasey received 753 rejection slips prior to the day his work was accepted. He later published 564 books.

The above examples are wonderfully inspiring to encourage us to persist with passion the dream or goal the Lord has placed in our hearts. It's easy to throw in the towel and walk away, but nothing great is ever accomplished with the "give up" plan. Giving up is too easy, and it's a shame that the majority of folks follow the tempting yield sign to this route.

I like what Lord Chesterfield said regarding persistence: "Aim at perfection in everything, though in most things it is unattainable. However, they who aim at it, and persevere, will come much nearer to it than those whose laziness and despondency make them give it up as unattainable." I agree, but I prefer the word "excellence" instead of perfection. Excellence seems more achievable because, at least, we're stretching ourselves and giving it our best shot, and that's what matters most, in my opinion.

The great William Carey (for whom the college I attended in Hattiesburg, MS was named) said, "I can plod. I can persevere in any definite pursuit. To this I owe everything."

Today's reading in Proverbs includes this golden nugget and is great advice for us to heed: "Look straight ahead, and fix your eyes on what lies before you. Mark out a straight path for your feet; then stick to the path" (Proverbs 4:25-26).

Michael Jordan, hailed as the greatest basketball player ever, gives his perspective on success: "I never looked at the consequences of missing a big shot. Why? Because when you think about the consequences you always think of a negative result." Jordan adds, "I realized that if I was going to achieve anything in life I had to be aggressive. I had to get out there and go for it." And look where this attitude of persistence took Jordan. He will always be known as one of the greatest basketball players of all time.

This principle of persistence is much like the one practiced by the Apostle Paul. He writes: "Forgetting the past and looking forward to what lies ahead, I strain to reach the end of the race and receive the prize for which God, through Christ Jesus, is calling us up to heaven" (Philippians 3:13-14). Paul was determined to keep his focus on what was in front of him; then not let anything or anyone distract him from moving forward in his desire to please God and share the gospel of Christ with the world. He lived and breathed his calling from God and persisted like crazy!

Have you joined the great Kingdom race God has called you to? Do you have the determination to persevere and finish the course? If you've made that decision, adopt the mindset of Winston Churchill and "never give up." Follow the path to which God has called you, and never look around to see what others are doing or how far along they are.

Look ahead *and* above, and whatever you do, persevere with passion!

Proverbs 4

1 My children, listen to me. Listen to your father's instruction. Pay attention and grow wise,

2 for I am giving you good guidance. Don't turn away from my teaching.

3 For I, too, was once my father's son, tenderly loved by my mother as an only child.

4 My father told me, "Take my words to heart. Follow my instructions and you will live.

5 Learn to be wise, and develop good judgment. Don't forget or turn away from my words.

6 Don't turn your back on wisdom, for she will protect you. Love her, and she will guard you.

7 Getting wisdom is the most important thing you can do! And whatever else you do, get good judgment.

8 If you prize wisdom, she will exalt you. Embrace her and she will honor you.

9 She will place a lovely wreath on your head; she will present you with a beautiful crown."

10 My child, listen to me and do as I say, and you will have a long, good life.

11 I will teach you wisdom's ways and lead you in straight paths.

12 If you live a life guided by wisdom, you won't limp or stumble as you run.

13 Carry out my instructions; don't forsake them. Guard them, for they will lead you to a fulfilled life.

14 Do not do as the wicked do or follow the path of evildoers.

15 Avoid their haunts. Turn away and go somewhere else,

16 for evil people cannot sleep until they have done their evil deed for the day. They cannot rest unless they have caused someone to stumble.

17 They eat wickedness and drink violence!

18 The way of the righteous is like the first gleam of dawn, which shines ever brighter until the full light of day.

19 But the way of the wicked is like complete darkness. Those who follow it have no idea what they are stumbling over.

20 Pay attention, my child, to what I say. Listen carefully.

21 Don't lose sight of my words. Let them penetrate deep within your heart,

22 for they bring life and radiant health to anyone who discovers their meaning.

23 Above all else, guard your heart, for it affects everything you do.

24 Avoid all perverse talk; stay far from corrupt speech.

25 Look straight ahead, and fix your eyes on what lies before you.

26 Mark out a straight path for your feet; then stick to the path and stay safe.

27 Don't get sidetracked; keep your feet from following evil.

Questions for Reflection:

1. What are your three top priorities in life? How good are you at sticking with them?

2. Have you abandoned a dream you've always wanted to attain? What is stopping you from trying again?

3. What caused you to become discouraged and give up on your dream in the first place?

4. In what ways can you honor God through your accomplishments?

Prayer:

Lord, forgive me for giving up so easily. Help me to persist and press on with what I feel like you want me to do. Help me to realize that I honor You when I accomplish the dreams You've placed in my heart. Thank you for giving me the desires of my heart (Psalm 37:4).

– Secret 5 –
Focus Fervently

Give me a man who says this one thing I do,
and not these fifty things I dabble in.
– Dwight L. Moody

Imagine for a moment that you are gazing down a long hallway. At the end awaits a nice prize, just for you—a bag on a pedestal containing one million dollars!

There is just one dilemma. This is not your typical corridor. The walls happen to be lined with powerful magnets, and you are wearing a metal jacket! Now you have a serious challenge on your hands, and the odds are somewhat stacked against you as you attempt to reach the bag.

As you make your way down the hall, you suddenly feel the tremendous force pulling from each side. It's so powerful that just one careless step could pull you off center.

You tell yourself, *I've got to stay focused—I have to concentrate*, realizing the only way you'll succeed is to stay in the middle. Once those magnets grab you, it's extremely difficult and next impossible to continue forward, much less pull free!

I believe the Christian life is similar to this hall of magnets—except the objective is far greater than a bag of cash. Our goal should always be to focus on Jesus Christ—to listen to and obey Him. Christ must be our focal point twenty-four hours a day, seven days a week.

Yet, we as Christians are constantly threatened by the powerful force of this world system and its flawed values. Satan tries every trick in his bag to keep us off-center—hoping he can distract us and pull us into sin and defeat.

In today's chapter of Proverbs, Solomon warns against falling into the trap of immorality, and he paints a bleak picture of both the present and the future of the person who deviates from God's path. For example, speaking of a sinful woman, he says, "So now, my sons, listen to me. Never stray from what I am about to say: Run from her! Don't go near the door of her house!" (Proverbs 5:7-8).

Evil is a powerful force—a vacuum that can pull you in long before you realize what has happened. Again and again, this chapter of Proverbs raises the red flag of danger. The result of disobedience, getting off-track, is "as bitter as poison, sharp as a double-edged sword" (v.4).

I know of only one way to stay centered. It's found in the words Jesus said to His disciples: "If any of you wants to be my follower, you must put aside your selfish ambition, shoulder your cross, and follow me" (Matthew 16:24). And in the Gospel of Luke, someone approaches Jesus about following Him, but this man wanted to first take care of a few family responsibilities at home—allowing temporal things distract him. But Jesus told him, "Anyone who puts a hand to the plow and then looks back is not fit for the Kingdom of God" (Luke 9:62). Keep your eyes zeroed in on the prize—the Lord Jesus Christ!

Focus fervently on HIM!

Proverbs 5

1 My son, pay attention to my wisdom; listen carefully to my wise counsel.

2 Then you will learn to be discreet and will store up knowledge.

3 The lips of an immoral woman are as sweet as honey, and her mouth is smoother than oil.

4 But the result is as bitter as poison, sharp as a double-edged sword.

5 Her feet go down to death; her steps lead straight to the grave.

6 For she does not care about the path to life. She staggers down a crooked trail and doesn't even realize where it leads.

7 So now, my sons, listen to me. Never stray from what I am about to say:

8 Run from her! Don't go near the door of her house!

9 If you do, you will lose your honor and hand over to merciless people everything you have achieved in life.

10 Strangers will obtain your wealth, and someone else will enjoy the fruit of your labor.

11 Afterward you will groan in anguish when disease consumes your body,

12 and you will say, "How I hated discipline! If only I had not demanded my own way!

13 Oh, why didn't I listen to my teachers? Why didn't I pay attention to those who gave me instruction?

14 I have come to the brink of utter ruin, and now I must face public disgrace."

15 Drink water from your own well—share your love only with your wife.

16 Why spill the water of your springs in public, having sex with just anyone?

17 You should reserve it for yourselves. Don't share it with strangers.

18 Let your wife be a fountain of blessing for you. Rejoice in the wife of your youth.

19 She is a loving doe, a graceful deer. Let her breasts satisfy you always. May you always be captivated by her love.

20 Why be captivated, my son, with an immoral woman, or embrace the breasts of an adulterous woman?

21 For the Lord sees clearly what a man does, examining every path he takes.

22 An evil man is held captive by his own sins; they are ropes that catch and hold him.

23 He will die for lack of self-control; he will be lost because of his incredible folly.

Questions for Reflection:

1. What common temptations seem to lure many away from the Lord?

2. What are three distractions that you personally have to deal with on a fairly regular basis?

3. What steps can you take to get back on center?

4. What are three primary requests that you would like to see God bring about in your life?

Prayer:

Lord, help me recognize those things that pull me away from You. Help me to focus on the eternal prize set before me—eternity with You.

– Secret 6 –
Learn Leadership

Pull the string, and it will follow you wherever you wish. Push it, and it will go nowhere at all.
–Dwight D. Eisenhower

There are so many concerns about leadership these days; namely, that there's a serious lack of it!

One of the key factors about being a leader is that you must be out front—ahead of the pack—to fulfill that role. And I've found that if you know what you want in life, and make a plan to go after it, the leader role becomes more automatic. It's like being lost in a jungle, and the leader is chopping away all the brush, crossing the dangerous streams, because he's discovered the secret way out. Other folks tend to follow someone like him, because *he* knows something *they* don't! But sadly, many people today simply don't know what they want or where they want to go in life. I've been there—it's boring.

During a question-answer session at one of my seminars, a gentleman asked, "Al, what do you think some key characteristics of effective leaders are today?"

After thinking about it, here's a bullet list of traits I came up with. I'm sure there are more you can add:

- Leaders are *thinkers*
- Leaders are *planners*
- Leaders are *visionaries*
- Leaders are *pullers*, not *pushers*
- Leaders set and achieve *goals*
- Leaders have a *positive attitude*
- Leaders practice *self-discipline*

• Leaders focus on what's *important*, over what's *urgent* (for example, time with family time over answering the phone.)
  • Leaders value *people over profits*
  • Leaders take *responsibility* for their decisions
  • Leaders are *learners*
  • Leaders see failure as a *learning experience*, not as a character flaw
  • Leaders take time to *re-energize*—through personal development
  • Leaders are good *listeners* (like doctors, they attempt to diagnose first, then treat)
  • Leaders are good *followers* (they remember that someone helped them get where they are now)
  • Leaders—TRUE leaders—are those who *trust Jesus Christ*, the Ultimate Leader and Creator of everything!

I'm sure you could come up with many more traits, but these are just a few I feel are essential to effective leadership.

Have you ever taken a self-inventory regarding the influence *you* have on others? Former pastor and success trainer, John Maxwell, teaches that leadership is simply *influence*! And from this standpoint, no one can truthfully say, "I am not a leader," because we are all influencing someone, somewhere, at some time, in some way, unless we're dead! (And even after death, our example continues to ripple for generations to come. Only God knows how long and far.)

How would you rate yourself on the above list? And by the way, these aren't just simply a matter of strengths or weaknesses in the "skills" area; all these traits involve character and attitude. We should never stop improving and growing as persons of influence and character.

True leaders are dynamic people—moving from better to best. Proverbs 6 contains the key ingredient for turning our visions into reality.

Leaders aren't just dreamers—they work on converting their dreams into reality. If they decide to put anything off, it would be procrastination. Solomon expresses it this way: "Don't put it off. Do it now! Don't rest until you do" (Proverbs 6:4).

Notice point seven and eight in the list: leaders practice *discipline*, and they focus on the *important* matters over the urgent ones.

That's exactly what Solomon is talking about when he says: "Take a lesson from the ants, you lazybones. Learn from their ways and be wise! Even though they have no prince, governor, or ruler to make them work, they labor hard all summer, gathering food for the winter. But you, lazybones, how long will you sleep? When will you wake up?" (Proverbs 6:6-9).

Solomon is saying that ants are sometimes smarter than humans, in that ants don't need someone walking behind, prodding them to get busy and keep moving. They are disciplined and they are always working on the important stuff. He's saying that we, as God's finest creation, need to *observe* the ants and *learn* from them. Sure, we need to stop and rest at times, but not all day long! We work, then rest, then work again. I believe we call this *balance*. An effective leader knows when to do both.

Jules Renard says, "Laziness is nothing more than the habit of resting before you get tired." Are you the kind that quits before you ever get started? That form of laziness is not highly favored in Scripture.

If great leaders frown upon laziness, as did King Solomon, there must be something said for the discipline of getting up, taking the bull by the horns, and being the kind of leaders and influencers God wants us as His followers to be.

Remember, ants are self-motivated—always looking ahead and planning. And surely, since we are created in God's own image, we should expect no less from ourselves!

We are all leaders, and we can certainly improve; the key is to become the best and most effective leaders we can be.

Proverbs 6

1 My child, if you co-sign a loan for a friend or guarantee the debt of someone you hardly know—

2 if you have trapped yourself by your agreement and are caught by what you said—

3 quick, get out of it if you possibly can! You have placed yourself at your friend's mercy. Now swallow your pride; go and beg to have your name erased.

4 Don't put it off. Do it now! Don't rest until you do.

5 Save yourself like a deer escaping from a hunter, like a bird fleeing from a net.

6 Take a lesson from the ants, you lazybones. Learn from their ways and be wise!

7 Even though they have no prince, governor, or ruler to make them work,

8 they labor hard all summer, gathering food for the winter.

9 But you, lazybones, how long will you sleep? When will you wake up? I want you to learn this lesson:

10 A little extra sleep, a little more slumber, a little folding of the hands to rest –

11 and poverty will pounce on you like a bandit; scarcity will attack you like an armed robber.

12 Here is a description of worthless and wicked people: They are constant liars,

13 signaling their true intentions to their friends by making signs with their eyes and feet and fingers.

14 Their perverted hearts plot evil. They stir up trouble constantly.

15 But they will be destroyed suddenly, broken beyond all hope of healing.

16 There are six things the Lord hates—no, seven things he detests:

17 haughty eyes, a lying tongue, hands that kill the innocent,

18 a heart that plots evil, feet that race to do wrong,

19 a false witness who pours out lies, a person who sows discord among brothers.

20 My son, obey your father's commands, and don't neglect your mother's teaching.

21 Keep their words always in your heart. Tie them around your neck.

22 Wherever you walk, their counsel can lead you. When you sleep, they will protect you. When you wake up in the morning, they will advise you.

23 For these commands and this teaching are a lamp to light the way ahead of you. The correction of discipline is the way to life.

24 These commands and this teaching will keep you from the immoral woman, from the smooth tongue of an adulterous woman.

25 Don't lust for her beauty. Don't let her coyness seduce you.

26 For a prostitute will bring you to poverty, and sleeping with another man's wife may cost you your very life.

27 Can a man scoop fire into his lap and not be burned?

28 Can he walk on hot coals and not blister his feet?

29 So it is with the man who sleeps with another man's wife. He who embraces her will not go unpunished.

30 Excuses might be found for a thief who steals because he is starving.

31 But if he is caught, he will be fined seven times as much as he stole, even if it means selling everything in his house to pay it back.

32 But the man who commits adultery is an utter fool, for he destroys his own soul.

33 Wounds and constant disgrace are his lot. His shame will never be erased.

34 For the woman's husband will be furious in his jealousy, and he will have no mercy in his day of vengeance.

35 There is no compensation or bribe that will satisfy him.

Questions for Reflection:

1. What are your "natural" leadership abilities?

2. How can you be a better "influencer" in your home? At work?

3. What skills do you need to develop—and in what areas will you make a commitment to improve?

4. What leadership traits did Jesus exhibit? How can you implement His traits into your own life? (Example: Being filled with the Holy Spirit).

Prayer:

Thank You, Lord, for the dream and vision You have placed in my heart. Help me to develop my abilities so they will reflect Your purpose for my life. May those I meet today know that I follow the Leader!

– Secret 7 –
Choose Cautiously

*When you have to make a choice and don't make it,
that in itself is a choice.* – William James

When a rocket at Cape Canaveral blasts off for the Moon or Mars, the NASA engineers don't just aim it in the right direction, cross their fingers, and hope for the best. It takes thousands of hours of detailed decisions, planning and preparation. If the rocket's trajectory path is off by just one degree, it could miss its destination by about a million miles, give or take a few. There are on-board computers constantly making mid-course corrections.

Because life is entirely unpredictable, we too must continually make the same type of mid-course corrections to our paths in life to work on. We can decide in one split second to change directions, and instantly, our course is altered. Our future is the result of the choices we make in the present.

The word *decide* comes from the Latin word meaning "to cut." So if you're unhappy and dissatisfied with your present circumstances, you can make the decision to "cut away" and create something new to work on! For example:

- If you don't like your job, change what you're doing at work, or else, look for another job.
- If you don't like your house, you can remodel it or move.
- If you don't like your marriage situation, you can decide to read some great books on how to

improve your relationship or get counseling and restore it.

Let me interject a quick note about the third bullet point. Sadly, many decide to go the divorce route because it appears to be the least painful option, but let me give you a tip: it's so much better to stay and work it out. Not that money should have anything to do with it, but I once heard someone humorously say, "Love is grand; divorce is a hundred grand!" Whether or not you are facing difficult times in your marriage, I highly recommend Dr. Gary Smalley's book *The DNA of Relationships*. It'll help you more than you can imagine, first, in your personal life, then in your marriage.

The Book of Proverbs talks a lot about choices—and there are hundreds of verses that contrast the results of foolish and wise decisions, advising us to choose cautiously.

Today's reading tells the story of a man who was lured by a married woman and, unfortunately, decided to take the destructive path: "He followed her at once, like an ox going to the slaughter or like a trapped stag, awaiting the arrow that would pierce its heart. He was like a bird flying into a snare, little knowing it would cost him his life" (Proverbs 7:22-23).

I think we can agree that every choice has a consequence. So how can we improve our decision-making? Here are some wise ideas from several Bible passages:

1. By using common sense (Proverbs 3:7).
2. By taking time to think before taking action (Philippians 4:8).
3. By an act of our will and a desire to *choose* the right path (Proverbs 3:5-6).
4. By using God's Word (the Bible) as our instruction manual and guide (Psalm 119:9-11).

5. By believing and sincerely trusting God to guide and help us (Hebrews 11:6).
6. By being *obedient* to God's word regardless of how we *feel* (John 15:10).
7. By spending some time in prayer about the decision and eagerly anticipate God's answer (Philippians 4:6; 1 Thessalonians 5:17-18).

We can't always change our circumstances, but we can certainly alter our response to them. Again, it's all about the choices we make.

Will we always take the right path? Not always, but God knows this. I've heard some people say, "I'm scared to make a decision because I might get off track and miss the Lord." Let me give you some good advice from one of my Bible teachers: "If you get off track, don't worry; He'll find you!" That's the way a true loving father is supposed to be, and God is every bit of that and more!

If we follow Solomon's advice and trust the Lord—plus, use the Bible as our guide—we can make better choices, and the chances of safely arriving at our chosen destination will be much greater.

So, here's our challenge: Decide to be prayerfully cautious and wise when making decisions. God is waiting to hear from you.

Proverbs 7

1 Follow my advice, my son; always treasure my commands.

2 Obey them and live! Guard my teachings as your most precious possession.

3 Tie them on your fingers as a reminder. Write them deep within your heart.

4 Love wisdom like a sister; make insight a beloved member of your family.

5 Let them hold you back from an affair with an immoral woman, from listening to the flattery of an adulterous woman.

6 I was looking out the window of my house one day

7 and saw a simpleminded young man who lacked common sense.

8 He was crossing the street near the house of an immoral woman. He was strolling down the path by her house

9 at twilight, as the day was fading, as the dark of night set in.

10 The woman approached him, dressed seductively and sly of heart.

11 She was the brash, rebellious type who never stays at home.

12 She is often seen in the streets and markets, soliciting at every corner.

13 She threw her arms around him and kissed him, and with a brazen look she said,

14 "I've offered my sacrifices and just finished my vows.

15 It's you I was looking for! I came out to find you, and here you are!

16 My bed is spread with colored sheets of finest linen imported from Egypt.

17 I've perfumed my bed with myrrh, aloes, and cinnamon.

18 Come, let's drink our fill of love until morning. Let's enjoy each other's caresses,

19 for my husband is not home. He's away on a long trip.

20 He has taken a wallet full of money with him, and he won't return until later in the month."

21 So she seduced him with her pretty speech. With her flattery she enticed him.

22 He followed her at once, like an ox going to the slaughter or like a trapped stag,

23 awaiting the arrow that would pierce its heart. He was like a bird flying into a snare, little knowing it would cost him his life.

24 Listen to me, my sons, and pay attention to my words.

25 Don't let your hearts stray away toward her. Don't wander down her wayward path.

26 For she has been the ruin of many; numerous men have been her victims.

27 Her house is the road to the grave. Her bedroom is the den of death.

Questions for Reflection:

1. What process do you use when making decisions?

2. List three life-altering choices you've made in the last three years.

3. Are you currently avoiding some very important decisions you need to act upon?

4. Pretend you had to face a big decision right now. What's the first step you'd take?

Prayer:

Lord, in the decisions I am facing, I ask for Your guidance and wisdom. Show me the path I should take and the doors through which I should walk. Help me make wise choices, and always use Your Word as my source of guidance.

– Secret 8 –
Crave Common Sense

Common sense is the genius of humanity.
– Wolfgang Von Gothe

It was Christmas Eve, 1971, in my hometown of Leakesville, Mississippi. One of my high school friends and I borrowed my dad's car and cruised around town. I "wisely" suggested to Bobby (not his real name) that we have a little fun and pop some firecrackers around the neighborhood.

So we bought six packs (that's 100 firecrackers in each unit, making the grand total 600) and unraveled them all into a paper grocery bag. Bobby sat on the passenger side as I drove. Positioning the bag between his feet, he was ready to ignite and toss each one out the window. Being extremely cold that night, he lowered his window only a couple of inches to keep the frigid air from rushing in.

After he exploded about five of them, I got to thinking *"Hey, what if one goes off in Dad's car? It could burn a hole somewhere and I'd be in big trouble."* I told Bobby, "We'd better rethink this whole idea and figure out something else to do."

Roughly sixteen seconds later, just as I was making a left turn, the unthinkable happened—Murphy (his last name "Law") jumped in the car with us. Then all of sudden, POW, POW, POW...times 595! The whole bag began exploding inside the car! Needless to say, it was a little loud—more like deafening! *But how in heaven's name could this have possibly happened?* I thought to myself. Here's what happened.

The lighter stick that Bobby was holding slipped from his hand right into the sack, and it started a massive chain reaction!

I panicked, opened *my* door, and jumped out of the car—while it was still moving, mind you—leaving Bobby to fight a losing battle. And you will NOT believe what happens next.

Common sense should have told him to get out, too. Instead, Bobby reaches down, grabs the bottom of the bag and attempts to shove the entire exploding inferno through the two-inch window space! I thought *"That was dumb. What made him think of that strategy?"*

When that plan failed, as hurriedly as he could, he crawled across the seat and rolled out of the car on MY SIDE—the car still moving. I'm thinking *"He had a door; why didn't he get out on his side? What was he thinking?"*

Well, thankfully, the car finally rolled to a stop in the ditch.

From our position—standing about 30 feet away—it looked like the inside of the car was an inferno, because my door was still open, which meant the roof light was still shining. Combined with the thick smoke, it looked like my Dad's car could have been in a Die Hard movie. Thank God, that wasn't the case!

Finally, it was all over—kind of. Still in basic shock, Bobby and I aired out the car as best we could, climbed back in and drove to his house a couple of blocks away.

We attempted to clean up the mess. Little pieces of paper were omnipresent. We pulled handfuls from under the seats. A thick layer of powder covered the dashboard.

But what concerned me the most were the permanent burn spots on the dash and upholstery. I thought to myself *"Well that's great! The only thing I'll get for Christmas this year is a BEATING!"*

Quietly, we sneaked into Bobby's room and turned on the light, and I couldn't believe what I saw next—

Bobby's long bangs were completely singed and curled backwards above his forehead! His eyelashes and eyebrows were all but vaporized! His shirt and jacket had tiny little burn spots all over—even his socks has holes as the sparks flew up his bell-bottom pants and down into his dingo boots! To this day, there's not one aspect of this trauma I don't recall without vivid detail.

So, what did we learn from this "hair-raising" experience?

First of all, stop and think before doing something so stinking stupid. We've should have known better and given more thought about the potential for a disaster!

Secondly, it's always good to exercise common sense. Bobby was a straight "A" student but didn't use his most valuable asset—common sense! Just look at how he reacted (cramming a bag of explosives through a 2-inch crack; getting out on *my* side, etc.). As for my part, I was the one responsible for coming up with the clever idea, which borders on pretty stupid!

Thirdly, sometimes circumstances can get out of our control. When they "blow up" and get out of hand, and there's nothing we can do about it, sometimes we just have to cut our losses and get out fast! "There's a time to stay and a time to get out!" (Maybe that should be in Ecclesiastes 3).

Proverbs speaks a great deal about common sense. If you carefully read the words of Solomon—especially in today's chapter—you'll learn that wisdom is the correct use of knowledge. Bobby and I didn't do that.

As for now, every time I see a "Fireworks" stand, I get a queasy feeling in the pit of my stomach, and that whole traumatic experience causes a flashback (no pun intended), reminding me: vehicles and fireworks are not a good combination! I won't do *that* again!

Proverbs 8

1 Listen as wisdom calls out! Hear as understanding raises her voice!

2 She stands on the hilltop and at the crossroads.

3 At the entrance to the city, at the city gates, she cries aloud,

4 "I call to you, to all of you! I am raising my voice to all people.

5 How naive you are! Let me give you common sense. O foolish ones, let me give you understanding.

6 Listen to me! For I have excellent things to tell you. Everything I say is right,

7 for I speak the truth and hate every kind of deception.

8 My advice is wholesome and good. There is nothing crooked or twisted in it.

9 My words are plain to anyone with understanding, clear to those who want to learn.

10 "Choose my instruction rather than silver, and knowledge over pure gold.

11 For wisdom is far more valuable than rubies. Nothing you desire can be compared with it.

12 I, Wisdom, live together with good judgment. I know where to discover knowledge and discernment.

13 All who fear the Lord will hate evil. That is why I hate pride, arrogance, corruption, and perverted speech.

14 Good advice and success belong to me. Insight and strength are mine.

15 Because of me, kings reign, and rulers make just laws.

16 Rulers lead with my help, and nobles make righteous judgments.

17 "I love all who love me. Those who search for me will surely find me.

18 Unending riches, honor, wealth, and justice are mine to distribute.

19 My gifts are better than the purest gold, my wages better than sterling silver!

20 I walk in righteousness, in paths of justice.

21 Those who love me inherit wealth, for I fill their treasuries.

22 The Lord formed me from the beginning, before he created anything else.

23 I was appointed in ages past, at the very first, before the earth began.

24 I was born before the oceans were created, before the springs bubbled forth their waters.

25 Before the mountains and the hills were formed, I was born –

26 before he had made the earth and fields and the first handfuls of soil.

27 "I was there when he established the heavens, when he drew the horizon on the oceans.

28 I was there when he set the clouds above, when he established the deep fountains of the earth.

29 I was there when he set the limits of the seas, so they would not spread beyond their boundaries. And when he marked off the earth's foundations,

30 I was the architect at his side. I was his constant delight, rejoicing always in his presence.

31 And how happy I was with what he created— his wide world and all the human family!

32 "And so, my children, listen to me, for happy are all who follow my ways.

33 Listen to my counsel and be wise. Don't ignore it.

34 Happy are those who listen to me, watching for me daily at my gates, waiting for me outside my home!

35 For whoever finds me finds life and wins approval from the Lord.

36 But those who miss me have injured themselves. All who hate me love death."

Questions for Reflection:

1. Name three unwise decisions have you made in the past. What would you do to change them?

2. What is the difference between wisdom and knowledge?

3. How do "God's wisdom" and "common sense" relate to each other?

4. How can you start today making better decisions? What will you use as your resource?

Prayer:

Lord, I admit the foolishness of my ways. Without You I am helpless and alone. May I learn to lean on Your understanding and trust You more each day.

– Secret 9 –
Fret Less Frequently

Worry is a thin stream of fear trickling through the mind. If encouraged, it cuts a channel into which all other thoughts are drained.
– Arthur Somers Roche

I recently discovered something interesting about fog. Some research was performed by the Bureau of Standards, and what it revealed was truly fascinating. The bureau discovered that dense fog, 100-feet deep, covering seven average city blocks—if compressed— could all be contained in an 8-ounce drinking glass!

This got me to thinking. I'm convinced that the majority of our problems are about the size of that small glass. Yet, worrying excessively over them expands their importance to such a degree that we become blind and helpless. This "fog" of fear and worry can effectivcly paralyze us.

Anxiety (better known as worry) is a real challenge for all of us. There have been numerous similar studies on the subject of worry, and most have discovered that people tend to fret over the following:

- Things that never happen (40%)
- Past events that can't be changed (30%)
- Needless worries over health (12%)
- Petty, miscellaneous worries (10%)
- Real, legitimate concerns (8%)

Another way to look at those statistics is that 92% of what we fear and fret over is a complete waste of time—pure fog, with practically no meaning or substance whatsoever!

The National Council on Aging study reveals older people worry far less today than they did 30 years ago. I believe it's because they've learned through experience that most anxieties aren't really worth the time and energy exerted to entertain them. It's a pure waste of time!

You may ask, "How do I know which is which? Which problems or challenges are real?"

First and foremost, we need to stop concerning ourselves with past events or situations over which we have zero control. To paraphrase the late Dale Carnegie, we need to "stop trying to water last year's crops with today's tears." Learn to let go of the past! We can't change it anyway; we can only *learn* from our mess-ups. We need to use our mistakes as "teachers" instead of "clubs" to beat ourselves up with.

A good example would be all the many marriages that have been wrecked by a husband or wife who continues to bring up the past mistakes of the other. Same goes for parents toward children. If you want to strain a relationship of any kind, just throw a previous blunder in the other person's face over and over.

Secondly, ask God to help you see your issues from *His* perspective. It's at this point you'll begin to realize how insignificant most of them really are. There's nothing wrong with being concerned about your job, finances, family, health, retirement, and safety. But be alert and don't confuse valid concerns with energy-draining worry.

There is only one thing we need to fear (the reverent kind)—and it is found in today's chapter. Solomon writes, "Fear of the Lord is the beginning of wisdom. Knowledge of the Holy One results in understanding" (Proverbs 9:10).

This "fear" does not mean we're to be scared or afraid of the Lord; rather it means we are to take Him seriously and have a reverence and awe for *who He is*! He is holy, powerful, loving and all-knowing! He's a big God, and we need to remind ourselves of who we worship. Our God is the Creator of the universe and everything that exists, which includes you and me! And if we look to Him, we'll worry less.

I want to mention something about "creation." Human beings can't "create" one single thing, especially from nothing! We must *have something* to *make something*. But God is the only One who can make something from absolutely nothing! We don't have the ability like God does to simply speak a word and have something appear out of thin air. But God can pull this off. He is the Creator. We have to be in awe of a God like that. In fact, He is the One, true God. There is NO other (See Exodus 20:3).

Since God is ruler over everything, and sovereign, let's refuse to allow normal, legitimate concerns to mushroom into mental anguish, life-damaging worry and desperation. Let's turn our cares and anxieties over to Jesus, who says, "The peace I give isn't like the peace the world gives. So don't be troubled or afraid" (John 14:27).

The following passage, Matthew 6:25-34, tells us all we need to know about the dangers of worry. This is so important that I ask you to read it slowly, with undistracted focus. Notice the difference in the way followers of Christ are supposed to trust God to take care of them, as compared to unbelievers:

25 That is why I tell you not to worry about everyday life—whether you have enough food and drink, or enough clothes to wear. Isn't life more than food, and your body more than clothing?

26 Look at the birds. They don't plant or harvest or store food in barns, for your heavenly Father feeds them. And aren't you far more valuable to him than they are?

27 Can all your worries add a single moment to your life?

28 And why worry about your clothing? Look at the lilies of the field and how they grow. They don't work or make their clothing,

29 yet Solomon in all his glory was not dressed as beautifully as they are.

30 And if God cares so wonderfully for wildflowers that are here today and thrown into the fire tomorrow, he will certainly care for you. Why do you have so little faith?

31 So don't worry about these things, saying, "What will we eat? What will we drink? What will we wear?"

32 These things dominate the thoughts of unbelievers, but your heavenly Father already knows all your needs.

33 Seek the Kingdom of God above all else, and live righteously, and he will give you everything you need.

34 So don't worry about tomorrow, for tomorrow will bring its own worries. Today's trouble is enough for today. –NLT

Have you ever thought about the fact that the same God who commands us not to kill, steal, murder, commit adultery, etc., also commands us *not to worry*! How is it that we think we can obey Him in some areas, but disobey Him in others? Disobedience is disobedience; it doesn't matter what it's regarding.

Hebrews 11:6 teaches us that "without faith it is impossible to please God." Faith is trusting in God; fretting is not trusting God. To put it another way, when we trust God, we're not going to worry; when we worry, we're not trusting God.

Allow God's perfect peace to replace your worry and negative fear. Just as that massive amount of fog can be contained in the small glass, so our faith, being as "small as a mustard seed," can expand to many times the size of a seven-city-block of fog.

So, step out of the "fog" of worry by focusing on God, who knows everything about you—past, present and future. You can calmly rest in the fact that God has everything under control.

Choose trust over worry, and learn to fret less!

Proverbs 9

1 Wisdom has built her spacious house with seven pillars.

2 She has prepared a great banquet, mixed the wines, and set the table.

3 She has sent her servants to invite everyone to come. She calls out from the heights overlooking the city.

4 "Come home with me," she urges the simple. To those without good judgment, she says,

5 "Come, eat my food, and drink the wine I have mixed.

6 Leave your foolish ways behind, and begin to live; learn how to be wise."

7 Anyone who rebukes a mocker will get a smart retort. Anyone who rebukes the wicked will get hurt.

8 So don't bother rebuking mockers; they will only hate you. But the wise, when rebuked, will love you all the more.

9 Teach the wise, and they will be wiser. Teach the righteous, and they will learn more.

10 Fear of the Lord is the beginning of wisdom. Knowledge of the Holy One results in understanding.

11 Wisdom will multiply your days and add years to your life.

12 If you become wise, you will be the one to benefit. If you scorn wisdom, you will be the one to suffer.

13 The woman named Folly is loud and brash. She is ignorant and doesn't even know it.

14 She sits in her doorway on the heights overlooking the city.

15 She calls out to men going by who are minding their own business.

16 "Come home with me," she urges the simple. To those without good judgment, she says,

17 "Stolen water is refreshing; food eaten in secret tastes the best!"

18 But the men don't realize that her former guests are now in the grave.

Questions for Reflection:

1. Try to recall a situation that caused you great anxiety and yet never came to pass. What did you end up doing about it?

2. Where do you draw the line between concern and worry?

3. How do you personally express a healthy "fear of the Lord"?

Prayer:

Lord, Your Word tells me to "fear not." I know You are holding me with Your strong hand and are instilling in me Your power and love. I thank You that in every trial You are my refuge and strength.

– Secret 10 –
Regard Reputation

Life is for one generation, a good name is forever.
– Japanese Proverb

I have a friend, a young Christian comedian, who is extremely funny and has the potential to become one of the best clean comedians in the country.

Once, however, as I listened to his routine—even though his material made people laugh—I felt that some portions could be interpreted as questionable or offensive and could potentially "cross the line" with our audience.

I discussed his routine with him privately and respectfully suggested, "If you want to move forward in your career, I suggest you eliminate those 'questionable' portions of your act." Thankfully, he listened with a humble, open mind and decided to remove them. I was relieved, because I really didn't want to hurt his feelings or discourage him. And as a result, his bookings increased, and I truly believe he avoided a tainted reputation. Our character and integrity are priceless treasures, and it doesn't take much to mar them.

As you read today's chapter in Proverbs, you'll find "People with integrity have firm footing, but those who follow crooked paths will slip and fall" (Proverbs 10:9). Later, in Chapter 22, Solomon tells us: "Choose a good reputation over great riches, for being held in high esteem is better than having silver or gold" (Proverbs 22:1). Mr. Truett Cathy, Founder of Chick-fil-A in Atlanta, Georgia, personally lives by, and founded his company on, the principle of this verse. This is why his company is so well respected and has the excellent reputation it enjoys to this day.

I want you to think for a moment about the contrast between these two names: Billy Graham and Adolf Hitler. What thoughts or emotions do each of these famous names conjure up? Well, of course, Billy Graham brings up good feelings because of the good he stands for; the other one, bad emotions! Very bad! So bad that I don't even want to repeat his name.

So, what about *your* reputation? What do others think when they hear *your* name? If you are a follower of Christ, your actions radiate to others either a positive or negative impression about Him, depending on how you're living. Our names and God's are forever linked, if we claim to follow Him. Put another way, *we* are the ones who carry God's reputation on this planet!

Proverbs 10 will encourage you to constantly guard your good name and reputation: "We all have happy memories of the godly, but the name of a wicked person rots away" (Proverbs 10:7).

Our reputation has a profound effect on every aspect of our lives: family, career, Christian testimony, and our future.

Our influence is like salt and light. Jesus says we are both "the salt of the earth" (Matthew 5:13) and "the light of the world" (v.14).

Notice the characteristics of each of these: Light provides warmth, eliminates darkness and gives vision. Salt preserves, enhances flavor, purifies and heals. It also makes us very thirsty! We as Christians are supposed to make people "thirsty for" a personal relationship with Him. Does your life make others thirst for Him?

But what if our conduct and influence haven't been very positive lately? What steps can we take to restore our reputation? Here are a few answers that might help:

1) Analyze. Take some time to think and evaluate where you may have gotten off track. Pray and ask God to show you. He's always willing and ready to help you, because you're His child.

2) Apologize. Confess and be open about your mistakes and short-comings, first to the Lord, and then to others you may have offended. If you have a core group of friends (which I highly recommend having), let them know where you got off-track and that you're trying to improve. They'll understand, because they have all been in your shoes at some point in their lives. Most people are very forgiving to those who say, "I'm sorry. I made a mistake. Will you forgive me?" Humility is admired far more than pride.

3) Actualize. In other words, act upon and put into practice what you're learning from your mistakes to avoid repeating them in the future. When you take action on correct information, your relationship with God and people will exponentially experience a positive, compounding effect.

Our reputation is like fine crystal glass—extremely fragile. Let's guard it with all our heart, and give others a good impression about Jesus by the way we live and conduct ourselves.

Regard your reputation!

Proverbs 10

1 The proverbs of Solomon: A wise child brings joy to a father; a foolish child brings grief to a mother.

2 Ill-gotten gain has no lasting value, but right living can save your life.

3 The Lord will not let the godly starve to death, but he refuses to satisfy the craving of the wicked.

4 Lazy people are soon poor; hard workers get rich.

5 A wise youth works hard all summer; a youth who sleeps away the hour of opportunity brings shame.

6 The godly are showered with blessings; evil people cover up their harmful intentions.

7 We all have happy memories of the godly, but the name of a wicked person rots away.

8 The wise are glad to be instructed, but babbling fools fall flat on their faces.

9 People with integrity have firm footing, but those who follow crooked paths will slip and fall.

10 People who wink at wrong cause trouble, but a bold reproof promotes peace.

11 The words of the godly lead to life; evil people cover up their harmful intentions.

12 Hatred stirs up quarrels, but love covers all offenses.

13 Wise words come from the lips of people with understanding, but fools will be punished with a rod.

14 Wise people treasure knowledge, but the babbling of a fool invites trouble.

15 The wealth of the rich is their fortress; the poverty of the poor is their calamity.

16 The earnings of the godly enhance their lives, but evil people squander their money on sin.

17 People who accept correction are on the pathway to life, but those who ignore it will lead others astray.

18 To hide hatred is to be a liar; to slander is to be a fool.

19 Don't talk too much, for it fosters sin. Be sensible and turn off the flow!

20 The words of the godly are like sterling silver; the heart of a fool is worthless.

21 The godly give good advice, but fools are destroyed by their lack of common sense.

22 The blessing of the Lord makes a person rich, and he adds no sorrow with it.

23 Doing wrong is fun for a fool, while wise conduct is a pleasure to the wise.

24 The fears of the wicked will all come true; so will the hopes of the godly.

25 Disaster strikes like a cyclone, whirling the wicked away, but the godly have a lasting foundation.

26 Lazy people are a pain to their employer. They are like smoke in the eyes or vinegar that sets the teeth on edge.

27 Fear of the Lord lengthens one's life, but the years of the wicked are cut short.

28 The hopes of the godly result in happiness, but the expectations of the wicked are all in vain.

29 The Lord protects the upright but destroys the wicked.

30 The godly will never be disturbed, but the wicked will be removed from the land.

31 The godly person gives wise advice, but the tongue that deceives will be cut off.

32 The godly speak words that are helpful, but the wicked speak only what is corrupt.

Questions for Reflection:

1. In what ways do you demonstrate that you are "salt" and "light" to the world?

2. What does your influence and reputation communicate to others?

3. If, for some reason, your good name has been tarnished in some way (whether in or out of your control), what steps can you take to begin the restoration process?

4. How would you like to be remembered? What legacy would you like to leave behind?

Prayer:

Father, I realize that as Your child, every action of my life reflects on You. Help me to be aware of the opportunities I have today to become a positive influence for You.

– Secret 11 –
Pass on Pride

*Do you wish people to speak well of you? Don't
speak well of yourself.*
– Blaise Pascal

We all know people who have a challenge with
greed, pride and selfishness. You know the type—the
one who's always extending his neck to get in the photo!

I heard a story about a very self-focused man at a
church picnic. After the prayer of thanks, he rushed up
to the front of the line, grabbed a plate and utensils,
then headed straight for the fried chicken platter.

After spying out the special pieces he wanted, he
claimed them by licking his finger and touching each
piece saying, "That one's mine, that one's mine, that
one's mine, and that one's mine!" Before he could fork
them to his plate, a little old lady standing next to him
also licked her finger and, touching those same pieces
said, "You can have it, you can have it, you can have it,
and you can have it!" Acting selfish doesn't have very
many pleasing, lasting benefits. Eventually, there will
be some repercussions to follow.

A prideful attitude emits negative vibes to others
and often returns similar results, just like an
unwelcome boomerang. The Apostle Paul says, "You
will always harvest what you plant" (Galatians 6:7b).

We can't get very far in life, at least the way God
wants us to, with a "me first" attitude. Why? Because
the Bible tells us: "Pride goes before destruction, and
haughtiness before a fall" (Proverbs 16:18).

That lesson was learned by a novice mountain
climber who, after an all-day ascent, reached a high

summit with his instructor. The moment they arrived at the peak, the jubilant student rushed past the guide and, standing tall with his hands lifted to the sky, shouted, "Alright! I made it, I made it!"

Quickly, the instructor grabbed him by the collar, jerked him down to the ground and said, "Be VERY careful! You can't do that! Once you get to the top, you have to kneel, because the wind will blow you over!"

What a great illustration! When we reach any God-inspired achievement in life, there's one clear thing we must remember: we should fall to our knees in humility and prayer, and thank the Lord for helping us get there. "For apart from me you can do nothing" (John 15:5).

In the chapter you're reading today, Solomon tells us: "Pride leads to disgrace, but with humility comes wisdom" (Proverbs 11:2).

The great evangelist Dwight L. Moody observed, "A man can counterfeit love, he can counterfeit hope, and all the other graces, but it is very difficult to counterfeit humility."

Have you ever noticed how pride seems to have that "lag" effect? To illustrate, let's say you wake up in the middle of the night, dying of thirst, and you must have something to drink. As you pass through the den on the way to the kitchen, your little toe just happens to catch the leg of the coffee table. At first, you look down at your pinkie toe—now bent at a 90 degree angle—and say to yourself *Oh, that didn't hurt all that...*, and before you can say *bad,* the pain reaches your brain and triggers a blood-curdling scream. Pride is a lot like that. At first it doesn't register, but then it kicks you, kind of like a horse's hoof to the solar plexus. (I saw that happen to a guy once on TV. I could feel the jolt where I was sitting on the couch!)

I heard someone say that "pride is the carbon monoxide of sin," meaning it sneaks up on you so subtly that you don't realize it until it's almost too late. We have to be on our guard against pride and arrogance.

The next time you become overconfident and think you're God's gift to the world, you might want to be on the lookout! There's a little old lady eyeballing your chicken; there's a coffee table eagerly waiting for your pinkie toe; there's a hoof in the spring-loaded position.

Take a pass on pride—because it's NOT always about YOU!

Proverbs 11

1 The Lord hates cheating, but he delights in honesty.

2 Pride leads to disgrace, but with humility comes wisdom.

3 Good people are guided by their honesty; treacherous people are destroyed by their dishonesty.

4 Riches won't help on the day of judgment, but right living is a safeguard against death.

5 The godly are directed by their honesty; the wicked fall beneath their load of sin.

6 The godliness of good people rescues them; the ambition of treacherous people traps them.

7 When the wicked die, their hopes all perish, for they rely on their own feeble strength.

8 God rescues the godly from danger, but he lets the wicked fall into trouble.

9 Evil words destroy one's friends; wise discernment rescues the godly.

10 The whole city celebrates when the godly succeed; they shout for joy when the godless die.

11 Upright citizens bless a city and make it prosper, but the talk of the wicked tears it apart.

12 It is foolish to belittle a neighbor; a person with good sense remains silent.

13 A gossip goes around revealing secrets, but those who are trustworthy can keep a confidence.

14 Without wise leadership, a nation falls; with many counselors, there is safety.

15 Guaranteeing a loan for a stranger is dangerous; it is better to refuse than to suffer later.

16 Beautiful women obtain wealth, and violent men get rich.

17 Your own soul is nourished when you are kind, but you destroy yourself when you are cruel.

18 Evil people get rich for the moment, but the reward of the godly will last.

19 Godly people find life; evil people find death.

20 The Lord hates people with twisted hearts, but he delights in those who have integrity.

21 You can be sure that evil people will be punished, but the children of the godly will go free.

22 A woman who is beautiful but lacks discretion is like a gold ring in a pig's snout.

23 The godly can look forward to happiness, while the wicked can expect only wrath.

24 It is possible to give freely and become more wealthy, but those who are stingy will lose everything.

25 The generous prosper and are satisfied; those who refresh others will themselves be refreshed.

26 People curse those who hold their grain for higher prices, but they bless the one who sells to them in their time of need.

27 If you search for good, you will find favor; but if you search for evil, it will find you!

28 Trust in your money and down you go! But the godly flourish like leaves in spring.

29 Those who bring trouble on their families inherit only the wind. The fool will be a servant to the wise.

30 The godly are like trees that bear life-giving fruit, and those who save lives are wise.

31 If the righteous are rewarded here on earth, how much more true that the wicked and the sinner will get what they deserve!

Questions for Reflection:

1. What aspects of your attitude and behavior could others interpret as being prideful?

2. Think about someone you know who's arrogant. Does that person inspire you to want to work with or socialize with him/her?

3. What lessons have you learned on the dangers of pride and conceit?

4. How does God humble those who act in prideful ways?

Prayer:

Lord, I acknowledge You as the Master of my thoughts. Help me to exercise the attitude of humility because I know it opens the door to Your blessings. Thank You for being the originator of every good and perfect gift.

– Secret 12 –
Sin Seldom

A tiny fly can choke a big man.
– Solomon Ben Gabirol

My wife, Carolyn, makes some of the best vegetable soup ever! I could enjoy it several times a week. It's especially tasty during the cold winter months.

Let's say I invite you over to experience some of her fabulous soup. We're dining at the table and, all of a sudden, we hear a buzzing sound. After circling the room a few times, Mr. Fly decides he wants to plop right smack in the middle of your bowl. What would be your response to that unwanted surprise? I doubt you'd rationalize saying, "Well, what's one little fly going to hurt? Just look at all that other good stuff in there—potatoes, meat, corn, beans, celery. I'm not going to let one tiny fly ruin my dinner!" I'm thinking you'd toss it all out and get a fresh bowl, because you know that flies are gross, hairy, filthy disease-carrying little former maggots!

Have you ever noticed how, as Christians, when we are complacent about sin in our lives, we start to have similar ridiculous conversations with God? Does this sound familiar? "Lord, I know what I'm doing is wrong, but You know I go to church, I'm honest, I read my Bible, I tithe my income, I help the poor..." blah, blah, blah! And the "fly" is still there!

What I'm about to say may seem a little foreign to you, but hang with me for a moment.

Do you realize that the moment you trusted Christ to be your Lord and Savior, you were transferred from the "sinner" to the "saint" group? That's right! You and

I are no longer labeled "sinners," but "saints," and we now have this new title because we've been rescued from the devil's family and adopted into God's family.

The person who chooses NOT to be a follower of Jesus Christ is considered a "sinner"—a rebellious, independent human being who wants to be in charge of his own life. But the person who follows Jesus Christ is considered a "saint"—one who is "set apart" and has given up control of his life to a new Lord and Master—Jesus Christ.

The word *sanctify* means, "To set apart for sacred use; consecrate." It means "to make holy." It is related to the word "saint," which means "one separated from the world and consecrated (set apart) to God; one holy by profession and by covenant; a believer in Christ" (See Psalm 16:3; Romans 1:7; 8:27; Philippians 1:1; Hebrews 6:10).

The moment we say "yes" to Jesus as our Lord, He makes us holy and blameless before Himself. How does He do that? I have no clue. I wish I understood it completely. He just does it and says that it's done, and I know that God doesn't lie. But I love the outcome—we are no longer guilty or accountable for the payment of our sin, because we have been forgiven and made right with God through Christ Jesus. That's why we call it "AMAZING GRACE!"

Notice how the Apostle Paul addressed the believers when he wrote to all the churches in the New Testament. Not once did he greet them as the "sinners at Ephesus," the "sinners at Corinth," or the "sinners at Philippi"; he addressed them all as "saints." And this is wonderful news! A "saint" is *who we are* in Christ. We've been adopted into the family of God, and now we are *His* holy children because of what Christ did for us on the cross!

Now since we are saints, do we still sin? Yes we do! But that's no longer our divine nature or bent. Imbedded within us is a divine desire to follow and obey Jesus. Our old life and desires have been replaced with Christ's life; and now we have a new *bent* toward the things of God. I like to think of this new nature within us as a heat-seeking missile, chasing after its mark—to honor and please God.

To add another metaphor, we've been given a divine "compass" with the needle of our hearts pointing "north" toward God. This "pull" within us is desires to please God. In fact, this new character is Christ Himself *living in us* (Galatians 2:20). And because of Christ, we now have the strength, freedom and the right to no longer be slaves to sin, but rather, overcomers of sin and slaves to God. We have been bought and purchased with the blood of Jesus, and now we belong to God.

King David, Solomon's father, is a good example of someone who sinned and blew it many times, yet God still considered him "a man after His own heart" (I Samuel 13:14). David still had to experience the consequences of his sin and bad choices, but God still loved and valued him as His child. And God never changes. No matter how badly you and I mess up—even as His followers—He feels the same about us!

As long as we're alive, we're going to struggle with temptation—that "gravitational pull" of independence and disobedience that tugs at every believer because of Satan's perpetual, lingering influence in this world.

In Ephesians 6, the Apostle Paul talks about the fight we're engaged in between the invisible forces of evil that remain in this earthly realm. You can count on this: Satan is working full time, doing all he can to drag us down and hinder our influence for God and his purpose.

But here's the great news: Satan can *harass* us, but he can *never possess* us, since we are in Christ and Christ is in us! We have the power and presence of the Holy Spirit living inside us to resist that pull. And because of His presence, we no longer have to obey sin (see Galatians 5:16-18).

As I said in chapter 1, God doesn't want us to avoid sin because of what *He* will do to us, but because of what *sin* does to us. It hurts us, His children, and He detests sin for that reason! He knows those little "flies" will contaminate our lives.

Proverbs 12 cautions us against the symptoms of rebelling against the Lord, which are manifested in the form of wickedness (v.2), idleness (v.11), jealousy (v.12), a quick temper (v.16) and deception (v.20); and this is just a "short list."

There are many more outcomes in Paul's letter to the Galatians: "When you follow the desires of your sinful nature, the results are very clear: sexual immorality, impurity, lustful pleasures, idolatry, sorcery, hostility, quarreling, jealousy, outbursts of anger, selfish ambition, dissension, division, envy, drunkenness, wild parties, and other sins like these. Let me tell you again, as I have before, that anyone living that sort of life will not inherit the Kingdom of God" (Galatians 5:19-21). Paul is referring to those whose lifestyle and desires are in rebellion against the Lordship of Jesus Christ.

Sin is systemic—that is, it doesn't affect just one aspect of your life; it infiltrates and sabotages all areas.

God's holy word is written to teach us to listen to His counsel and to strengthen our immunity to sin and its effects. Solomon instructs, "Fools think they need no advice, but the wise listen to others" (Proverbs 12:15).

Although our *relationship* to God can never be broken, our *fellowship* can be. We will always be His children, but we may not always be in harmony with Him, just like we experienced with our earthly parents. God offers a divine plan to remove the impurities from our lives. It's called confession. If we confess our sin and turn from it, we'll be cleansed and restored back to fellowship with God (I John 1:9).

Just as a little fly can ruin your soup, don't allow sin (acting independently toward God) to ruin your life and your effectiveness for God's kingdom.

When we're full of God, we will sin less.

Proverbs 12

1 To learn, you must love discipline; it is stupid to hate correction.

2 The Lord approves of those who are good, but he condemns those who plan wickedness.

3 Wickedness never brings stability; only the godly have deep roots.

4 A worthy wife is her husband's joy and crown; a shameful wife saps his strength.

5 The plans of the godly are just; the advice of the wicked is treacherous.

6 The words of the wicked are like a murderous ambush, but the words of the godly save lives.

7 The wicked perish and are gone, but the children of the godly stand firm.

8 Everyone admires a person with good sense, but a warped mind is despised.

9 It is better to be a nobody with a servant than to be self-important but have no food.

10 The godly are concerned for the welfare of their animals, but even the kindness of the wicked is cruel.

11 Hard work means prosperity; only fools idle away their time.

12 Thieves are jealous of each other's loot, while the godly bear their own fruit.

13 The wicked are trapped by their own words, but the godly escape such trouble.

14 People can get many good things by the words they say; the work of their hands also gives them many benefits.

15 Fools think they need no advice, but the wise listen to others.

16 A fool is quick-tempered, but a wise person stays calm when insulted.

17 An honest witness tells the truth; a false witness tells lies.

18 Some people make cutting remarks, but the words of the wise bring healing.

19 Truth stands the test of time; lies are soon exposed.

20 Deceit fills hearts that are plotting evil; joy fills hearts that are planning peace!

21 No real harm befalls the godly, but the wicked have their fill of trouble.

22 The Lord hates those who don't keep their word, but he delights in those who do.

23 Wise people don't make a show of their knowledge, but fools broadcast their folly.

24 Work hard and become a leader; be lazy and become a slave.

25 Worry weighs a person down; an encouraging word cheers a person up.

26 The godly give good advice to their friends; the wicked lead them astray.

27 Lazy people don't even cook the game they catch, but the diligent make use of everything they find.

28 The way of the godly leads to life; their path does not lead to death.

Questions for Reflection:

1. Take a moment to identify a "fly" (action or attitude) that has "spoiled your soup" recently.

2. In your observation, how has one sin messed up the lives of someone you know, or even yourself?

3. What attitude can you ask the Lord to help you with that might be hindering your fellowship with Him?

Prayer:

Lord, I've allowed some unpleasing mindsets and attitudes to invade my life. Today I am asking You to cleanse my heart, soul and body, and restore me into a sweet fellowship with You. Only then will I experience your peace.

– Secret 13 –
Dream Daringly

You can't depend on your eyes when your imagination is out of focus.
– Mark Twain

Let's say I called you on the phone from the airport and told you that "I know where a buried treasure chest is down in south Mississippi. I really don't want it, so I'm going to give it to you, if that's okay. I'm in a hurry to catch a flight, so I only have just enough time to give you directions only once on how to get there and where you'll find the treasure."

What's the first thing you would scramble for? Besides panicking and thinking I'd lost my mind, if you were smart, you'd grab a pen and paper and start writing every detail.

In my friend's, Steven Scott's, bestselling book, *Mentored by a Millionaire*, he teaches a skill called "Dream Conversion." Steve developed this process in order to teach others how to "convert" a dream that seems utterly impossible into an actuality. In essence, he says that when it comes to pursuing dreams, most people never create and write down a specific plan of action—no step-by-step written strategy—to "convert" their dreams into reality. As a result, their vision remains only an idea, put on the shelf, and never realized.

Such people remind me of a hunter in the woods who closes his eyes and shoots several times—BLAM! BLAM! BLAM!—then says, "Boy, I sure hope something good runs into that!" That's not an effective strategy. You've got to have a better plan! Steve's Dream

Conversion helps you achieve your ambitions at an accelerated rate.

It's a sad fact, but most people give up on their dreams before they even start. Why is this? I believe it's because 1) they think they won't reach them, and 2) they listen to someone else who spouts off "it's impossible" or "it can't be done."

But starting today, I want you to give up on giving up. If God has given you the go ahead on a dream or great ambition, then go for it, no matter what anyone else says—especially the pessimists!

As Paul reminds us, "For I can do everything with the help of Christ who gives me the strength I need" (Philippians 4:13).

Solomon says, "It is pleasant to see dreams come true, but fools will not turn from evil to attain them" (Proverbs 13:19).

While pursuing your dreams, I'd like to suggest seven strategies that work for me, and hopefully they'll inspire you as well:

1. **FOCUS—Focus on your wants, not your "don't wants."** It's counterproductive to think about what you don't want—because that's exactly what you'll end up getting! For example, if I say, "Don't think of a roach," what image just popped in your head? That's right! A ROACH! In the same way, when you train yourself to think about what you DO WANT, your mind will also go to work on making that very thing happen. Notice what the Apostle Paul writes: "Finally, brothers, whatever is true, whatever is noble, whatever is right, whatever is pure, whatever is lovely, whatever is admirable...think about such things" (Philippians 4:8 NIV). In this passage, Paul's focus was on the positive, not the negative.

2. **CREATIVITY—Learn to exercise your creativity.** God is creative, and so are we—because

we're made by Him and in His image. He fashioned us to be creative! I realize that some use this gift more than others, but we all possess it. And when we practice creative thinking (by asking the questions: who, what, when, where, how and why), we are far more likely to achieve our goals much faster.

3. **PRIORITY—Make your dreams a top priority.** Think about them each day. Keep them in the forefront of your mind. Maybe write your dreams in a journal or on your computer. Another idea would be to take a picture of something that reminds you of your dream, and keep that photo on your phone or tablet so you can look at it several times a day.

4. **BELIEF—You must believe your dreams are achievable**. Hebrews 11:1 says, "Without faith it is impossible to please God," and it's also impossible to achieve a goal without belief. James Allen said it well in his little book *As a Man Thinketh*: "He who cherishes a beautiful vision, a lofty vision in his heart, will one day realize it."

5. **PRIVACY—Keep your dreams private**. In other words, be a little protective of your goals and don't divulge your plans to just anybody. Share them with only a select few who are positive, encouraging and supportive of you and what you're trying to accomplish. They will inspire you, as well as help you be accountable, and become more motivated.

6. **ACTION—Take action daily (even if it's a small task) toward your dream**. Assuming you're in good health, you could walk 250 miles, if you take one step at a time. It may take you several days, but it's doable. The same principle applies to your ambitions. They may seem impossible, but

when you divide any dream into tiny steps, it's simply a matter of time before you accomplish that dream. What once seemed impossible is now possible!

7. **GUIDANCE—Ask God for direction**. Ask Him to give you wisdom and guidance; ask God if this desire is *His will*. Is it second nature for you to consult Him before moving forward? As Solomon reminds us: "Trust in the Lord with all your heart; do not depend on your own understanding. Seek his will in all you do, and he will direct your paths" (Proverbs 3:5-6).

God is not out to squash our desires. We are His children, and it's okay for us to ask Him for what we want and need. Sometimes He'll say "yes," other times He'll say "no," and many times He'll say "hang on" because the timing is not right. I like what Solomon says: "Hope deferred makes the heart sick, but when dreams come true, there is life and joy" (Proverbs 13:12).

The most important thing is that we should pursue God FIRST, then our aspirations. This way, our priorities are in alignment with Him, and our dreams will coincide with His will.

Dream big for the Kingdom!

Proverbs 13

1 A wise child accepts a parent's discipline; a young mocker refuses to listen.

2 Good people enjoy the positive results of their words, but those who are treacherous crave violence.

3 Those who control their tongue will have a long life; a quick retort can ruin everything.

4 *Lazy people want much but get little, but those who work hard will prosper and be satisfied.*

5 *Those who are godly hate lies; the wicked come to shame and disgrace.*

6 *Godliness helps people all through life, while the evil are destroyed by their wickedness.*

7 *Some who are poor pretend to be rich; others who are rich pretend to be poor.*

8 *The rich can pay a ransom, but the poor won't even get threatened.*

9 *The life of the godly is full of light and joy, but the sinner's light is snuffed out.*

10 *Pride leads to arguments; those who take advice are wise.*

11 *Wealth from get-rich-quick schemes quickly disappears; wealth from hard work grows.*

12 *Hope deferred makes the heart sick, but when dreams come true, there is life and joy.*

13 *People who despise advice will find themselves in trouble; those who respect it will succeed.*

14 *The advice of the wise is like a life-giving fountain; those who accept it avoid the snares of death.*

15 *A person with good sense is respected; a treacherous person walks a rocky road.*

16 *Wise people think before they act; fools don't and even brag about it!*

17 *An unreliable messenger stumbles into trouble, but a reliable messenger brings healing.*

18 *If you ignore criticism, you will end in poverty and disgrace; if you accept criticism, you will be honored.*

19 *It is pleasant to see dreams come true, but fools will not turn from evil to attain them.*

20 *Whoever walks with the wise will become wise; whoever walks with fools will suffer harm.*

21 *Trouble chases sinners, while blessings chase the righteous!*

22 Good people leave an inheritance to their grandchildren, but the sinner's wealth passes to the godly.

23 A poor person's farm may produce much food, but injustice sweeps it all away.

24 If you refuse to discipline your children, it proves you don't love them; if you love your children, you will be prompt to discipline them.

25 The godly eat to their hearts' content, but the belly of the wicked goes hungry.

Questions for Reflection:

1. What dreams do you feel God has inspired you to achieve? Are you afraid to pursue them? If you are, then why?

2. Name two or three dreams you've given up on or placed on the back-burner.

3. If you had only six months left to live, how would your desires and dreams change?

4. What specific actions are you going to take toward achieving your godly ambitions?

Prayer:

Lord, thank You for giving me a vision for my family, my career, my spiritual life and my future. I pray that as I fulfill Your purpose, it will enable me to serve others and bring honor to You.

– Secret 14 –
Plant Purposefully

Sure, you can find a cheaper burger;
but then you gotta eat it!
—Texas Burger slogan

Earl Nightingale used to tell the story about a farmer who had some rich, fertile soil. He conducted an experiment and planted two seeds: one of corn and the other nightshade, a deadly poison.

The farmer dug two holes in the earth, placed the seeds, covered them up and faithfully watered them.

Many days later, the two plants emerged from the soil—one corn, the other a poisonous plant. The farmer reaped exactly what he had sown. The land will always return what is planted. It's a basic principle of sowing and reaping, and our lives are no different from that farmland.

Think about your mind, for example. It is tender, fertile "soil," but you must be careful what you allow into it. The mind will return wickedness in the same abundance as it will goodness. It will produce what is sown—positive or negative, wisdom or foolishness, peace or conflict, faith or fear.

Our subconscious minds are much more delicate than our conscious minds. I like to think of our subconscious as film (before the digital age) in a camera, and our eyes (the conscious mind) are like the camera lens. The film doesn't care what the camera lens focuses upon; it just simply receives and sears the image.

Whether you choose to meditate on the good things of God or the evil Satan tosses your way, both will leave imprints on your mind and affect you in a positive or negative manner. The old adage is true: "We become what we think about most of the time." Solomon reminds us, "For as he thinks within himself, so he is" (Proverbs 23:7 –NASB).

In Proverbs we see the cause-effect, planting-reaping principle again and again. For example, in today's reading, Solomon says: "If you plot evil, you will be lost; but if you plan good, you will be granted unfailing love and faithfulness" (Proverbs 14:22). In other words, if you sow into evil, the reaping will be aimless wandering; but if you sow good things, you will reap love, faithfulness and all the outcomes associated with goodness.

Here are three concrete facts we need to remember about sowing and reaping:

1. We always reap **what** we sow. We can't plant peppers and reap sweet potatoes.
2. We always reap **more** than we sow. The plant is always bigger than the seed.
3. We always reap **later** than we sow. The harvest comes later and is simply a matter of T-I-M-E. In time, good will come to the godly, and evil to the wicked; sometimes quickly, but the results always come later.

The law of sowing and reaping applies whether we are conscious of it or not. We are told, "There is a path before each person that seems right, but it ends in death" (Proverbs 14:12). This applies to *everyone*! No one is exempt from this law. Some may argue, "Well that doesn't really apply to me and my situation." That would be like saying "gravity doesn't work the same way in Africa like it does in America." Here's a clue for you: *yes it does*! And I can tout with certainty that you would *not* be willing to stand on a twenty-story building and give it a test run!

On the positive side, the Apostle Paul exhorts, "So don't get tired of doing what is good. Don't get discouraged and give up, for we will reap a harvest of blessing at the appropriate time" (Galatians 6:9).

Remember: reaping is a natural result of what we sow! There's no getting around it.

Regarding our minds, let's be cautious about what we allow to be planted in them. If we sow, we *will* reap. Decide to plant God's word in your mind; then discover the beautiful outcome that awaits you.

Proverbs 14

1 A wise woman builds her house; a foolish woman tears hers down with her own hands.

2 Those who follow the right path fear the Lord; those who take the wrong path despise him.

3 The talk of fools is a rod for their backs, but the words of the wise keep them out of trouble.

4 An empty stable stays clean, but no income comes from an empty stable.

5 A truthful witness does not lie; a false witness breathes lies.

6 A mocker seeks wisdom and never finds it, but knowledge comes easily to those with understanding.

7 Stay away from fools, for you won't find knowledge there.

8 The wise look ahead to see what is coming, but fools deceive themselves.

9 Fools make fun of guilt, but the godly acknowledge it and seek reconciliation.

10 Each heart knows its own bitterness, and no one else can fully share its joy.

11 The house of the wicked will perish, but the tent of the godly will flourish.

12 There is a path before each person that seems right, but it ends in death.

13 Laughter can conceal a heavy heart; when the laughter ends, the grief remains.

14 Backsliders get what they deserve; good people receive their reward.

15 Only simpletons believe everything they are told! The prudent carefully consider their steps.

16 The wise are cautious and avoid danger; fools plunge ahead with great confidence.

17 Those who are short-tempered do foolish things, and schemers are hated.

18 The simpleton is clothed with folly, but the wise person is crowned with knowledge.

19 Evil people will bow before good people; the wicked will bow at the gates of the godly.

20 The poor are despised even by their neighbors, while the rich have many "friends."

21 It is sin to despise one's neighbors; blessed are those who help the poor.

22 If you plot evil, you will be lost; but if you plan good, you will be granted unfailing love and faithfulness.

23 Work brings profit, but mere talk leads to poverty!

24 Wealth is a crown for the wise; the effort of fools yields only folly.

25 A truthful witness saves lives, but a false witness is a traitor.

26 Those who fear the Lord are secure; he will be a place of refuge for their children.

27 Fear of the Lord is a life-giving fountain; it offers escape from the snares of death.

28 A growing population is a king's glory; a dwindling nation is his doom.

29 Those who control their anger have great understanding; those with a hasty temper will make mistakes.

30 A relaxed attitude lengthens life; jealousy rots it away.

31 Those who oppress the poor insult their Maker, but those who help the poor honor him.

32 The wicked are crushed by their sins, but the godly have a refuge when they die.

33 Wisdom is enshrined in an understanding heart; wisdom is not found among fools.

34 Godliness exalts a nation, but sin is a disgrace to any people.

35 A king rejoices in servants who know what they are doing; he is angry with those who cause trouble.

Questions for Reflection:

1. What kind of good "seeds" are you planting in your own life?

2. Describe the differences between wise and foolish people.

3. What good deed have you "sown" into someone's life, but haven't yet seen the harvest? Does not seeing results discourage you and cause you to stop planting?

Prayer:

Thank you, Lord, for every seed You have placed into my hand—talent, time and treasure. Today, I am making a commitment to plant the good in my mind and share what I learn with others. And I need your help to do this; for without you, I'm nothing.

– Secret 15 –
Banish Bellyaching

*No pessimist ever discovered the secrets of the stars,
or sailed to an uncharted land, or opened a new
heaven to the human spirit.*
– Helen Keller

Late one afternoon, a delivery man pulled his truck up to a ram-shackled house on a rural road in East Texas.

On the rambling front porch sat an old pipe-smoking farmer in his rocking chair. A few feet away lay his bloodhound dog, just moaning and whining.

"Excuse me, sir," began the concerned young man, "What's the matter with your dog? Why is he fussing like that?"

The old man, with an attitude of total indifference and country slang, replied, "Oh, he's layin' on a nail."

"Well, why doesn't he just get up?" the delivery man wanted to know.

Shrugging his shoulders, the old man answered, "Well, I guess he ain't hurtin' bad enough!"

I've met folks who are just like that pitiful dog—whining and complaining about how tough things are and how life is treating them, but they won't take the initiative to "get off the nail" and make any attempt to change their circumstances. I'll have to admit, these folks are hard to help. In fact, if they invested as much time looking for answers as they do complaining, most of their problems would scurry away like a frightened puppy.

But instead, they'd rather throw a "pity party," and get all bent out of shape when no one shows up! Life is way too short to hang around these people—the negative clan and complainers. I'll take the optimistic group any day!

Solomon begins this chapter by talking about "gentle words" and challenges us to live with optimism and joy. We learn that what resides on the inside is reflected on the outside: "A glad heart makes a happy face; a broken heart crushes the spirit" (Proverbs 15:13).

Have you ever noticed that when we give (and receive) that which is uplifting, positive and affirming, we become energized? "A cheerful look brings joy to the heart; good news makes for good health" (Proverbs 15:30).

Solomon wasn't only a wise king; in this verse he comes across like a psychologist, telling us if we stop infusing our lives with the *negative* and replace it with the *positive*, we could have a physical regeneration—i.e., more energy! Even more, he says, "for the happy heart, life is a continual feast" (Proverbs 15:15).

If we want things to improve in our lives and relationships, we must follow the Apostle Paul's advice and redirect our attention from ourselves onto others.

He says we should "encourage each other and build each other up...And remember to live peaceably with each other...Encourage those who are timid. Take tender care of those who are weak. Be patient with everyone. See that no one pays back evil for evil, but always try to do good to each other and to everyone else. Always be joyful" (1 Thessalonians 5:11, 13-16).

Tucked away in these verses is the key to happiness: "Encourage one another—be patient with everyone."

To put it bluntly, let's get rid of our "I" problem and start focusing on others.

It's time to banish your bellyaching and get off the nail!

Proverbs 15

1 A gentle answer turns away wrath, but harsh words stir up anger.

2 The wise person makes learning a joy; fools spout only foolishness.

3 The Lord is watching everywhere, keeping his eye on both the evil and the good.

4 Gentle words bring life and health; a deceitful tongue crushes the spirit.

5 Only a fool despises a parent's discipline; whoever learns from correction is wise.

6 There is treasure in the house of the godly, but the earnings of the wicked bring trouble.

7 Only the wise can give good advice; fools cannot do so.

8 The Lord hates the sacrifice of the wicked, but he delights in the prayers of the upright.

9 The Lord despises the way of the wicked, but he loves those who pursue godliness.

10 Whoever abandons the right path will be severely punished; whoever hates correction will die.

11 Even the depths of Death and Destruction are known by the Lord. How much more does he know the human heart!

12 Mockers don't love those who rebuke them, so they stay away from the wise.

13 A glad heart makes a happy face; a broken heart crushes the spirit.

14 A wise person is hungry for truth, while the fool feeds on trash.

15 For the poor, every day brings trouble; for the happy heart, life is a continual feast.

16 It is better to have little with fear for the Lord than to have great treasure with turmoil.

17 A bowl of soup with someone you love is better than steak with someone you hate.

18 A hothead starts fights; a cool-tempered person tries to stop them.

19 A lazy person has trouble all through life; the path of the upright is easy!

20 Sensible children bring joy to their father; foolish children despise their mother.

21 Foolishness brings joy to those who have no sense; a sensible person stays on the right path.

22 Plans go wrong for lack of advice; many counselors bring success.

23 Everyone enjoys a fitting reply; it is wonderful to say the right thing at the right time!

24 The path of the wise leads to life above; they leave the grave behind.

25 The Lord destroys the house of the proud, but he protects the property of widows.

26 The Lord despises the thoughts of the wicked, but he delights in pure words.

27 Dishonest money brings grief to the whole family, but those who hate bribes will live.

28 The godly think before speaking; the wicked spout evil words.

29 The Lord is far from the wicked, but he hears the prayers of the righteous.

30 A cheerful look brings joy to the heart; good news makes for good health.

31 If you listen to constructive criticism, you will be at home among the wise.

32 If you reject criticism, you only harm yourself; but if you listen to correction, you grow in understanding.

33 Fear of the Lord teaches a person to be wise; humility precedes honor.

Questions for Reflection:

1. What previous negative experiences (things you refuse to let go of) should you eliminate from your conversation?

2. Do others view you as an optimist or a pessimist? Where's the proof?

3. What part of your attitude needs fine-tuning?

4. Specifically, what can you do in the days ahead to influence others to experience more joy in their lives?

Prayer:

Lord, please help me as I place my problems and difficulties at Your feet. No longer will I dwell in discouragement and despair. Help my words bring encouragement, hope and optimism to those I meet today.

– Secret 16 –
Forego Facade

Be what you are. This is the first step toward
becoming better than you are.
– Julius Charles Hare

We all know a few folks who are more style than substance. They attempt to make us think they are really something they're not—trying to use the "fake it 'til you make it" formula for getting ahead.

I once heard Denis Waitley, one of the greatest inspirational and personal development coaches of our time, share a story about a young man who was promoted to his first management position in the company where he worked.

On the first day at his new job he was given a very impressive corner office with a mahogany credenza and a marvelous view. Closing the door, he walked around in circles trying to feel like an executive, wondering how he was going to handle the promotion he'd attained with his gift of gab and a great golf swing.

He wanted to make sure everyone respected him from the very start because he felt a little insecure of his ability to perform.

About that time there was a knock on the door. In a flash, he leaped behind his desk, quickly sank back into his high-back chair, grabbed the telephone, and in a deep voice announced, "Come right in!"

When the man entered, the new manager motioned for him to have a seat and said, "Just a minute, I'll be right with you; I'm in the middle of an important call."

Ignoring the gentleman who was now seated in front of him, the new executive spoke into the phone receiver, "Yes, sir. I appreciate your confidence in me, and I accept full responsibility for both those new territories. You can count on a dramatic increase in sales." Then, after a pause, concluded, "You're welcome, sir. Thanks for the call."

Next, he looked up at the visitor and confidently inquired, "Now what can I do for you?"

The visitor smiled and replied, "Well, I just came to connect your telephone!"

Attempting to impress through deceit is a sure sign of low self-esteem. Trying to be something you're not always backfires. You are eventually exposed—often with great embarrassment.

In Proverbs 16, Solomon warns of the dangers of deception. He says, "It is better to be poor and godly than rich and dishonest" (Proverbs 16:8).

Climbing the ladder of success through devious means is a prelude to disaster. After all, "Pride goes before destruction, and haughtiness before a fall" (Proverbs 16:18).

Sometimes younger, starting-out comedians ask me about what it takes to be funny and successful as a comedian. And I simply give them my opinion: "Be yourself; be genuine. Don't copy anyone else. You are unique, so act that way. Just be YOU!" I've discovered that being myself—the way God made me—is a much easier way to come up with funny material. I can be inspired by others without copying them.

Although it's important to be authentic with yourself and others, it's especially so with God. He's the One who knows all about you (see Psalm 139). Your friends can be hoodwinked for a while, but God NEVER can. Sooner or later, the buzzards will find the corpse, that is, you WILL be found out!

Every action of your life and motive of your heart will be an open book. As the Apostle Paul states, "Yes, each of us will have to give a personal account to God" (Romans 14:12).

Focus on being your true self—the person God made you to be.

It takes a lot less energy to be real!

Proverbs 16

1 We can gather our thoughts, but the Lord gives the right answer.

2 People may be pure in their own eyes, but the Lord examines their motives.

3 Commit your work to the Lord, and then your plans will succeed.

4 The Lord has made everything for his own purposes, even the wicked for punishment.

5 The Lord despises pride; be assured that the proud will be punished.

6 Unfailing love and faithfulness cover sin; evil is avoided by fear of the Lord.

7 When the ways of people please the Lord, he makes even their enemies live at peace with them.

8 It is better to be poor and godly than rich and dishonest.

9 We can make our plans, but the Lord determines our steps.

10 The king speaks with divine wisdom; he must never judge unfairly.

11 The Lord demands fairness in every business deal; he sets the standard.

12 A king despises wrongdoing, for his rule depends on his justice.

13 The king is pleased with righteous lips; he loves those who speak honestly.

14 The anger of the king is a deadly threat; the wise do what they can to appease it.

15 When the king smiles, there is life; his favor refreshes like a gentle rain.

16 How much better to get wisdom than gold, and understanding than silver!

17 The path of the upright leads away from evil; whoever follows that path is safe.

18 Pride goes before destruction, and haughtiness before a fall.

19 It is better to live humbly with the poor than to share plunder with the proud.

20 Those who listen to instruction will prosper; those who trust the Lord will be happy.

21 The wise are known for their understanding, and instruction is appreciated if it's well presented.

22 Discretion is a life-giving fountain to those who possess it, but discipline is wasted on fools.

23 From a wise mind comes wise speech; the words of the wise are persuasive.

24 Kind words are like honey—sweet to the soul and healthy for the body.

25 There is a path before each person that seems right, but it ends in death.

26 It is good for workers to have an appetite; an empty stomach drives them on.

27 Scoundrels hunt for scandal; their words are a destructive blaze.

28 A troublemaker plants seeds of strife; gossip separates the best of friends.

29 Violent people deceive their companions, leading them down a harmful path.

30 With narrowed eyes, they plot evil; without a word, they plan their mischief.

31 Gray hair is a crown of glory; it is gained by living a godly life.

32 It is better to be patient than powerful; it is better to have self-control than to conquer a city.

33 We may throw the dice, but the Lord determines how they fall.

Questions for Reflection:

1. What experiences have you had with people who exaggerate their self-importance? Inwardly, what are you thinking as they do this?

2. What lessons regarding the dangers of vanity and pride can be applied to your own life?

3. If you knew you would face God tomorrow at noon, what changes would you start making today?

Prayer:

Lord, You made me and You know me better than I know myself. Help me to stop fooling myself and allow You to be Yourself through me.

– Secret 17 –
Prize People

*The richest man in the world is not the one who has
the first dollar he ever earned.
It is the man who still has his best friend.*
– Martha Mason

When we get into debt over our heads or have cash flow problems, it becomes pretty tempting to shift our focus to thinking more about money than we do people. However, we often fail to realize it is through others that we earn our living. Think about it! The very thing that brings us all we ever need is what we often sabotage. To illustrate the point, let me a share a story.

Every August, Stumpy and his wife, Martha, went to the State Fair. One of the annual attractions was a quick ride over the fairgrounds in a small open-cockpit airplane.

Each year, Stumpy would say, "Martha, I'd like to ride in that there airplane!" And every time Martha would respond the same way: "I know, Stumpy, but that airplane ride costs ten dollars—and ten dollars is ten dollars!"

Finally, one year when the now-elderly couple was attending the fair, Stumpy turned to his wife and remarked, "Martha, I'm 71 years old. If I don't ride that plane this year, I may never get another chance."

Martha repeated what she had always maintained: "Stumpy, that airplane ride costs ten dollars, and ten dollars is ten dollars."

The pilot overheard their little argument and, eager to drum up business, said, "Folks, I'll make you a deal. I will take you both up for a ride. If you can stay quiet for the entire flight and not say one word, I won't charge you. But if you talk, it's ten dollars."

Stumpy and Martha quickly agreed and up they went. The pilot did all kinds of twists, turns, rolls, flips and dives, but not a word was heard. He did all his tricks the second time, yet total silence.

When they landed, the pilot turned to Stumpy and remarked, "Mister, I did everything I could to get you to yell out, but you didn't!"

Stumpy replied, "Well, sir, I was going to say something when Martha fell out, but ten dollars is ten dollars!"

As you read Solomon's wisdom, you'll find that relationships are far more valuable than riches. Instead of being a *taker*, he tells us to be a *giver*. In today's chapter, he writes, "A friend is always loyal, and a brother is born to help in time of need" (Proverbs 17:17).

Godly wealth is the result of being diligent, trustworthy and servant-minded. Money must never be the driving, motivating factor. Solomon gives this example: "A wise slave will rule over the master's shameful sons and will share their inheritance" (Proverbs 17:2).

The "wise slave" wasn't looking for wealth; he was only trying to do the right thing. The inheritance was an unexpected bonus.

Many get confused and often misquote what the Bible says about money, saying, "Money is the root of all evil." Not true. Paul says, "For the **love** of money is the root of all evil" (I Timothy 6:10). He is not saying that **money** is the root; he's saying it's the *love* of money. There's a huge difference. How so?

I know people who are not wealthy who have the love of money. Just ask them what they would do if they won the lottery. You'll learn quickly where their heart is aimed. I also know several wealthy people who have a ton of financial resources and a high net worth, but you won't find one hint of the "love of money." They understand that money is something to *use*, not *love*. They treat money like gasoline. Gasoline is simply a product that gets you where you want to go. Stupid is the person who hangs around the service station all day, hugging the pumps.

People who understand wealth and where it really originates use money as an instrument for good, making the world a better place. Bottom line: the proper or improper use of money is a heart-related issue, and that's what the Apostle Paul is talking about.

Don't become so caught up in chasing dollars that you brush aside what's truly important. You can't put a price tag or monetary value on the important things—life, family and friends.

Jesus tells us to "love your neighbor as yourself" (Matthew 22:39). It is through *others* that we receive many of life's greatest gifts. Therefore, prize people over profit.

Proverbs 17

1 A dry crust eaten in peace is better than a great feast with strife.

2 A wise slave will rule over the master's shameful sons and will share their inheritance.

3 Fire tests the purity of silver and gold, but the Lord tests the heart.

4 Wrongdoers listen to wicked talk; liars pay attention to destructive words.

5 Those who mock the poor insult their Maker; those who rejoice at the misfortune of others will be punished.

6 Grandchildren are the crowning glory of the aged; parents are the pride of their children.

7 Eloquent speech is not fitting for a fool; even less are lies fitting for a ruler.

8 A bribe seems to work like magic for those who give it; they succeed in all they do.

9 Disregarding another person's faults preserves love; telling about them separates close friends.

10 A single rebuke does more for a person of understanding than a hundred lashes on the back of a fool.

11 Evil people seek rebellion, but they will be severely punished.

12 It is safer to meet a bear robbed of her cubs than to confront a fool caught in folly.

13 If you repay evil for good, evil will never leave your house.

14 Beginning a quarrel is like opening a floodgate, so drop the matter before a dispute breaks out.

15 The Lord despises those who acquit the guilty and condemn the innocent.

16 It is senseless to pay tuition to educate a fool who has no heart for wisdom.

17 A friend is always loyal, and a brother is born to help in time of need.

18 It is poor judgment to co-sign a friend's note, to become responsible for a neighbor's debts.

19 Anyone who loves to quarrel loves sin; anyone who speaks boastfully invites disaster.

20 The crooked heart will not prosper; the twisted tongue tumbles into trouble.

21 It is painful to be the parent of a fool; there is no joy for the father of a rebel.

22 A cheerful heart is good medicine, but a broken spirit saps a person's strength.

23 The wicked accept secret bribes to pervert justice.

24 Sensible people keep their eyes glued on wisdom, but a fool's eyes wander to the ends of the earth.

25 A foolish child brings grief to a father and bitterness to a mother.

26 It is wrong to fine the godly for being good or to punish nobles for being honest!

27 A truly wise person uses few words; a person with understanding is even-tempered.

28 Even fools are thought to be wise when they keep silent; when they keep their mouths shut, they seem intelligent.

Questions for Reflection:

1. What value do you place on your family and personal and work relationships?

2. What blessings have you experienced just for being a friend to someone in need?

3. How do you show through your life and actions that you prioritize people above things?

Prayer:

Heavenly Father, thank You for the loving, faithful people You have placed in my life. Help me to realize that nothing I can attain on earth is more valuable than my love for You, and then others.

– Secret 18 –
Try Trinkets

The entire population of the universe, with one trifling exception, is composed of others.
– John Andrew Holmes

Bill was a nice guy, but had a challenge connecting with people. He knew a great many folks on a shallow level, but had very few close friends.

One day, while chatting with an acquaintance, Bill noticed his friend's attention wandering. He appeared bored out of his mind, his thoughts a thousand miles away as he was looking out the window.

Bill got to thinking about this and made an embarrassing discovery. He realized that he had only been talking about *himself.* Conversations were nothing more than an opportunity to vent his opinions and to brag about all that was going on in *his* life. Before the other person could slide a word in, Bill was mentally reloading, getting ready to talk even more about himself. It finally dawned on him why he had so few friends. He wasn't being a true friend to the other person and had little or no interest in others and their opinions.

Right then, he made the decision to change.

Knowing how hard it was to break old habits, he decided he needed a little extra help. So he stopped by a toy store and purchased a marble. From that point forward, every time Bill chatted with someone, he would hold the marble in his hand as a tangible reminder to think about the other person. He let *them* do most of the talking, and always attempted to steer the conversation back to them and their interests.

Before long, Bill no longer had a problem making friends.

That simple "magic marble" made scores of friends for him. It taught him to stop thinking about himself all the time. But an unexpected benefit came to him as well: he found that he was actually becoming genuinely concerned about others. And when that happened, he started an avalanche of friendships!

Solomon was well aware of this problem centuries ago. He writes, "Fools have no interest in understanding; they only want to air their own opinions" (Proverbs 18:2).

We've always heard: "Knowledge is power." But how can we learn anything if we are doing all the speaking? I like what the Texas senator, Sam Rayburn, once said: "When you're talking, you ain't learning."

In this chapter of Proverbs we are cautioned: "What a shame, what folly, to give advice before listening to the facts!" (Proverbs 18:13). And we are also told: "Intelligent people are always open to new ideas. In fact, they look for them" (v.15). We should not only be open to new *ideas*, but open to *people*. Many times it's from *them* that great ideas come!

Since most individuals are self-centered, you won't make many friends by constantly promoting yourself. The key is to listen carefully and sincerely to what others are saying. Show a genuine interest by asking questions—not just one or two, but as many as you can! Good questions can lead to rewarding friendships, plus you'll make people feel valued, which is what we all crave.

Now, first thing tomorrow, do yourself and others a big favor; try a trinket—go get your magic marble!

Proverbs 18

1 A recluse is self-indulgent, snarling at every sound principle of conduct.

2 Fools have no interest in understanding; they only want to air their own opinions.

3 When the wicked arrive, contempt, shame, and disgrace are sure to follow.

4 A person's words can be life-giving water; words of true wisdom are as refreshing as a bubbling brook.

5 It is wrong for a judge to favor the guilty or condemn the innocent.

6 Fools get into constant quarrels; they are asking for a beating.

7 The mouths of fools are their ruin; their lips get them into trouble.

8 What dainty morsels rumors are—but they sink deep into one's heart.

9 A lazy person is as bad as someone who destroys things.

10 The name of the Lord is a strong fortress; the godly run to him and are safe.

11 The rich think of their wealth as an impregnable defense; they imagine it is a high wall of safety.

12 Haughtiness goes before destruction; humility precedes honor.

13 What a shame, what folly, to give advice before listening to the facts!

14 The human spirit can endure a sick body, but who can bear it if the spirit is crushed?

15 Intelligent people are always open to new ideas. In fact, they look for them.

16 Giving a gift works wonders; it may bring you before important people!

17 Any story sounds true until someone sets the record straight.

18 Casting lots can end arguments and settle disputes between powerful opponents.

19 It's harder to make amends with an offended friend than to capture a fortified city. Arguments separate friends like a gate locked with iron bars.

20 Words satisfy the soul as food satisfies the stomach; the right words of a person's lips bring satisfaction.

21 Those who love to talk will experience the consequences, for the tongue can kill or nourish life.

22 The man who finds a wife finds a treasure and receives favor from the Lord.

23 The poor plead for mercy; the rich answer with insults.

24 There are "friends" who destroy each other, but a real friend sticks closer than a brother.

Questions for Reflection:

1. In your daily conversations, which word is more frequently used: "I" or "you?"
2. What steps will you take today to become a good listener and to better concentrate on the other person's interests?
3. When you pray, do you only talk about *your* needs to the Lord, or do you focus on just simply being with Him?

Prayer:

Father help me to turn my attention from myself and be genuinely interested in others. Let me listen with an understanding heart and become a friend of those in need.

– Secret 19 –
Talk Truth

What upsets me is not that you lied to me, but that from now on I can no longer believe you.
–Friedrich Wilhelm Neitzsche

It was April in Denver. Jason had just turned sixteen and his dad gave him the keys to a brand new red convertible. Boy was he proud of that car!

The next day at school, his buddies were begging him to take them for a spin. So four of them took off during lunch break and hit the streets.

Unfortunately, they had such a great time cruising around that they were more than one hour late getting back to class.

Mrs. Smith, their teacher, was extremely annoyed.

"Where in the world have you boys been?" she demanded.

"Oh, Mrs. Smith," replied the smooth-tongued Jason, "we're very sorry. The reason we are late is because we had a flat tire and had to fix it."

The teacher said, "Well, I want you four boys to stay a few minutes after class"—and she went on with her lesson.

When the final bell rang and the rest of the students filed out of the room, Mrs. Smith informed them, "To make up for being late I am going to give you pop quiz—and you'll only have to answer one question."

That sounded reasonable enough to the tardy teens. Then the teacher gave them the rules. "I want each of you to sit in a different corner of the room, facing away from each other."

When they obliged, she said, "Now take out a piece of paper and answer this question: Which tire was flat?" All four boys flunked the test!

Lying isn't a new trick. It began when Satan, in the form of a serpent, lied to Eve about her right to eat from the Tree of Knowledge. Then Eve lied to Adam to entice him to also eat of the forbidden fruit. And later, Adam lied (i.e., tried to lie) to God concerning his own role in the matter.

People who lie always think they can get away with it and won't be discovered. But that's like trying to sneak a sunrise past a rooster! You WILL hear about it!

I have reminded my children many times: "A lie is a short cut, and any time you take the *short cut*, you always get *cut short*!" The words of Solomon are true: "A false witness will not go unpunished, nor will a liar escape" (Proverbs 19:5).

Sadly, lying has become a part of the fabric of our society. A friend says, "I'll reimburse you tomorrow," and the politician promises, "If I'm elected...." Then there are the whoppers that result in public trials for perjury.

Christians aren't immune from the temptation to shade the truth. I even heard about a preacher who announced at the end of a service that the next Sunday he would deliver a sermon on *The Dangers of Lying*. "In preparation, I want everyone to read Psalm 155."

The following Sunday, the minister began his message by asking, "Everyone who has read the 155th Psalm, please raise your hand." Nearly half the congregation signaled they had.

"You are just the people I need to preach to," exclaimed the preacher. "There is no Psalm 155!" Quite a little trick, but the point hit home.

Be on guard and constantly ask yourself, "Do I pass the test of truthfulness?"

You never have to study for the *Truth Test*!

Proverbs 19

1 It is better to be poor and honest than to be a fool and dishonest.

2 Zeal without knowledge is not good; a person who moves too quickly may go the wrong way.

3 People ruin their lives by their own foolishness and then are angry at the Lord.

4 Wealth makes many "friends"; poverty drives them away.

5 A false witness will not go unpunished, nor will a liar escape.

6 Many beg favors from a prince; everyone is the friend of a person who gives gifts!

7 If the relatives of the poor despise them, how much more will their friends avoid them. The poor call after them, but they are gone.

8 To acquire wisdom is to love oneself; people who cherish understanding will prosper.

9 A false witness will not go unpunished, and a liar will be destroyed.

10 It isn't right for a fool to live in luxury or for a slave to rule over princes!

11 People with good sense restrain their anger; they earn esteem by overlooking wrongs.

12 The king's anger is like a lion's roar, but his favor is like dew on the grass.

13 A foolish child is a calamity to a father; a nagging wife annoys like a constant dripping.

14 Parents can provide their sons with an inheritance of houses and wealth, but only the Lord can give an understanding wife.

15 A lazy person sleeps soundly—and goes hungry.

16 Keep the commandments and keep your life; despising them leads to death

17 If you help the poor, you are lending to the Lord—and he will repay you!

18 Discipline your children while there is hope. If you don't, you will ruin their lives.

19 Short-tempered people must pay their own penalty. If you rescue them once, you will have to do it again.

20 Get all the advice and instruction you can, and be wise the rest of your life.

21 You can make many plans, but the Lord's purpose will prevail.

22 Loyalty makes a person attractive. And it is better to be poor than dishonest.

23 Fear of the Lord gives life, security, and protection from harm.

24 Some people are so lazy that they won't even lift a finger to feed themselves.

25 If you punish a mocker, the simpleminded will learn a lesson; if you reprove the wise, they will be all the wiser.

26 Children who mistreat their father or chase away their mother are a public disgrace and an embarrassment.

27 If you stop listening to instruction, my child, you have turned your back on knowledge.

28 A corrupt witness makes a mockery of justice; the mouth of the wicked gulps down evil.

29 Mockers will be punished, and the backs of fools will be beaten.

Questions for Reflection:

1. Do you believe God differentiates between a "little white lie" and a "big lie?"

2. Are there areas of your life where you need to ask forgiveness for watering down the truth?

3. Whom do you consider to be a role model for truthfulness? Can you be such a person?

Prayer:

Lord, help me guard my words. Remove deceit from my heart and lies from my lips. Today, may I be a true example of Your truth and a representative of Your righteousness. I pray this in the name of Christ, amen.

– Secret 20 –
Acquire Ambitions

If you don't have goals,
you will forever work for those who do.
– Brian Tracy

As an entertainer in the comedy field, one of my lifetime goals was to meet the late, Bob Hope.

In 1990, after talking with a dear friend (Lulu Roman of the famous TV show, *Hee Haw*), things began to unfold, and I was invited to perform for a Bob Hope-sponsored fundraiser in Beaumont, Texas to benefit physically handicapped children.

I was overwhelmed with excitement! I thought, *This is it! I'm finally going to meet Mr. Hope!* Unfortunately, it wasn't to be. I was so close but, for whatever reason, many of us were kept a good distance from the show business legend.

Fortunately, I was invited back the next year, and this time I wasn't going to let this opportunity pass me by a second time. I was determined to meet him—no matter what!

I mapped out a plan and strategy. I stayed alert to every possible situation where I might have a chance encounter. I was scouting and plotting, nearly on the verge of stalking!

But to make a long story short, the moment came! It happened! We linked up after the show and I finally got to meet him face to face and shake his hand! And I've got the pictures to prove it. I had accomplished one of my long-time dreams.

Oddly enough, my routine was the only one Mr. Hope saw that night, because he was there just a short time before heading off to another engagement in Nashville with Dolly Parton. At the end of my segment, he walked over to me and said, "I really enjoyed your routine. You're a real nut!" Wow! That was pretty awesome, coming straight from the comedic star himself!

In another scenario, I've always wanted to meet former President George W. Bush. And I did! Granted, I had to stand in line from 5:00am till 10:30am at a local bookstore, waiting for him to autograph my copy of his new book. But I was determined to meet him, and it totally made my day!

These goals may not seem like a big deal to you, but remember, they aren't *your* goals; they're *mine*, and they were very important to me. And that's the key: accomplishing what's important to *you*!

Achieving a goal or dream is a lot of fun. But it's not really the accomplishing of the goal that's really rewarding—it's what you have to *become* to achieve that dream. To acquire something different, you yourself have to become something bigger.

Many people don't have goals and I can't understand why. If you are the kind who isn't very ambitious, or don't have any dreams, I suggest you make it your number one priority and turn that around. The most important thing we can do is to ask the Lord to show us what He wants us to do. We are His children, and He is not playing hide-and-seek with us. He wants to accomplish His will through us. It wouldn't hurt to ask Him what His will is. I think He'll clue you in.

Most people deep down would love to reach their objectives, but they're not exactly willing to work hard enough to make anything happen. Maybe the goal isn't big enough to motivate them. Maybe they don't know how. Maybe they're just too lazy and don't really care. Who really knows?

Proverbs 20:4 tells us: "If you are too lazy to plow in the right season, you will have no food at the harvest."

Look, if you're having trouble with having any worthy ambitions, don't give up; there is hope. Earlier, in Proverbs 4:25, Solomon gives six keys to reaching your goal (I've broken the verse down):

- *Look straight ahead*
- *Fix your eyes on what lies before you*
- *Mark out a straight path for your feet*
- *Then stick to the path and stay safe*
- *Don't get sidetracked*
- *Keep your feet from following evil*

In other words:

- Have clear vision and direction
- Focus and concentrate
- Plan and organize
- Be committed and persistent
- Avoid distractions
- Have pure motives and do the right thing

Our talents and abilities can only take us so far. To experience success the way God wants us to, we must be in submission to His Lordship. As the Apostle Paul asks: "Have you lost your senses? After starting your Christian lives in the Spirit, why are you now trying to become perfect by your own human effort?" (Galatians 3:3). Paul is saying that we *started* by faith and we must *continue* our journey of growth by faith (i.e., daily trusting God for everything).

Today, maybe we can learn from the wisdom of Solomon—to give God our plans and realize that "it is the Lord who directs our steps" (Proverbs 20:24). If we make it our number one goal to obey the Lord, the rest of our dreams and achievements will fall in line with *His* plans.

Be the kind of goal-achiever *God* wants you to be.

Proverbs 20

1 Wine produces mockers; liquor leads to brawls. Whoever is led astray by drink cannot be wise.

2 The king's fury is like a lion's roar; to rouse his anger is to risk your life.

3 Avoiding a fight is a mark of honor; only fools insist on quarreling.

4 If you are too lazy to plow in the right season, you will have no food at the harvest.

5 Though good advice lies deep within a person's heart, the wise will draw it out.

6 Many will say they are loyal friends, but who can find one who is really faithful?

7 The godly walk with integrity; blessed are their children after them.

8 When a king judges, he carefully weighs all the evidence, distinguishing the bad from the good.

9 Who can say, "I have cleansed my heart; I am pure and free from sin?"

10 The Lord despises double standards of every kind.

11 Even children are known by the way they act, whether their conduct is pure and right.

12 Ears to hear and eyes to see—both are gifts from the Lord.

13 If you love sleep, you will end in poverty. Keep your eyes open, and there will be plenty to eat!

14 The buyer haggles over the price, saying, "It's worthless," then brags about getting a bargain!

15 Wise speech is rarer and more valuable than gold and rubies.

16 Be sure to get collateral from anyone who guarantees the debt of a stranger. Get a deposit if someone guarantees the debt of a foreigner.

17 Stolen bread tastes sweet, but it turns to gravel in the mouth.

18 Plans succeed through good counsel; don't go to war without the advice of others.

19 A gossip tells secrets, so don't hang around with someone who talks too much.

20 If you curse your father or mother, the lamp of your life will be snuffed out.

21 An inheritance obtained early in life is not a blessing in the end.

22 Don't say, "I will get even for this wrong." Wait for the Lord to handle the matter.

23 The Lord despises double standards; he is not pleased by dishonest scales.

24 How can we understand the road we travel? It is the Lord who directs our steps.

25 It is dangerous to make a rash promise to God before counting the cost.

26 A wise king finds the wicked, lays them out like wheat, then runs the crushing wheel over them.

27 The Lord's searchlight penetrates the human spirit, exposing every hidden motive.

28 Unfailing love and faithfulness protect the king; his throne is made secure through love.

29 The glory of the young is their strength; the gray hair of experience is the splendor of the old.

30 Physical punishment cleanses away evil; such discipline purifies the heart.

Questions for Reflection:

1. What dreams do you have for your family? Your career? Your spiritual life?

2. Do you have a written plan with specific action steps to make them a reality?

3. What are you doing to make certain your goals are aligned with God's will? Are *your* goals *God's* goals?

4. Are you asking God to be a part of *your* plans, or are you aligning yourself with *His* plan for your life?

Prayer:

Lord, according to Your Word, if I delight myself in You, You will give me the desires of my heart. But my plans are nothing without Your direction. I am placing my desires and plans into Your hands. Lead, guide and direct—and I will give You all the praise.

– Secret 21 –
Manage Motives

Whatever you love most, be it sports, pleasure,
business, or God, that is your god!
– Billy Graham

One summer night after dinner, when I was about twelve years old, I didn't have anything in particular to do, so I decided I'd go outside and sit on the front door steps.

Right as I sat down, something caught the corner of my eye. I looked down the sidewalk to my right and noticed a little dog I'd never seen before making his way toward me. He looked pretty hungry.

Feeling sorry for him, I went back into the kitchen, grabbed a leftover piece of chicken-fried steak from the table and returned to the steps. I tossed the steak toward him, and when I did, he seemed to have that look on his face: *You've got to be kidding! This is for me?*

Needless to say, he was pretty happy as he began chomping away at the entre.

But then I got this weird idea (I'm known for these). I wanted to try something that never worked previously with my own dogs. As he was eating, I waited until he was half way through, then I called out, "Here, boy. Come here!" I wanted to see if he'd leave the steak and come to me.

To my astonishment, he immediately abandoned the steak and ran up to me, as if to say, *Yep, what do you want?*

I was blown away! I never had this happen before. My pets' attitude was more like, *Not so fast. I know you're my master and everything, but you're nuts if you think I'm leaving this treat for you!*

I just wanted to know: *Did this little starving dog love* me *more than the* steak? It sure seemed that way. So I patted him on the head and let him get back to eating.

The Lord loves us and wants to provide for us. But sometimes I think we tend to love the *blessings* more than the *Blesser*. And He knows when we confuse the two. Deep down, we know it, too. If we get out of balance, He may "call us from the steak."

As Solomon explains in today's chapter, God sees more than just our outward actions. He knows what's occurring inside: "People may think they are doing what is right, but the Lord examines the heart" (Proverbs 21:2). God sees our motives, no matter what we're up to. He wants our love for Him to originate from pure hearts. He wants us to be godly in all we do and say. According to His Word, "Whoever pursues godliness and unfailing love will find life, godliness, and honor" (Proverbs 21:21).

In the New Testament, there is a story of a rich young ruler who came to Jesus, asking, "Good teacher, what should I do to get eternal life?" (Luke 18:18).

Jesus responded, "Sell all you have and give the money to the poor, and you will have treasure in heaven. Then come, follow me" (v.22). The Lord was testing the man's true devotion.

So how did the ruler respond? He bowed his head and walked away, choosing the *blessings* over the *Blesser*.

I've often thought about what might have occurred if the young ruler had answered in this manner: "Okay, Lord. I'll do it! When do I start?" There's no way to know for sure what Jesus would have said next. He could have said, "Great, thank you for your obedience. Your treasure will be great in Heaven. Now leave everything and come follow me." Or, He might have said, "Great, thank you for your obedience. You don't have to give it all away, but I wanted to see if you were willing. I want you to be sensitive to the needs of others and help those in need; and don't be a hoarder. Bless others as I have blessed you, and your treasure will be great in Heaven." This young man would have been a true example of what it means to have one's priorities in order. In my opinion, I think the latter would have happened.

Regardless, the Lord wants our hearts—our motives and deepest desires—to be totally centered on *Him*, not His *handouts*.

Is Jesus at the top of your "love list?" Do you love Him more than anything else? If you do, you'll truly love and serve others, and your motives will be well-managed.

Proverbs 21

1 The king's heart is like a stream of water directed by the Lord; he turns it wherever he pleases.

2 People may think they are doing what is right, but the Lord examines the heart.

3 The Lord is more pleased when we do what is just and right than when we give him sacrifices.

4 Haughty eyes, a proud heart, and evil actions are all sin.

5 Good planning and hard work lead to prosperity, but hasty shortcuts lead to poverty.

6 Wealth created by lying is a vanishing mist and a deadly trap.

7 Because the wicked refuse to do what is just, their violence boomerangs and destroys them.

8 The guilty walk a crooked path; the innocent travel a straight road.

9 It is better to live alone in the corner of an attic than with a contentious wife in a lovely home.

10 Evil people love to harm others; their neighbors get no mercy from them.

11 A simpleton can learn only by seeing mockers punished; a wise person learns from instruction.

12 The Righteous One knows what is going on in the homes of the wicked; he will bring the wicked to disaster.

13 Those who shut their ears to the cries of the poor will be ignored in their own time of need.

14 A secret gift calms anger; a secret bribe pacifies fury.

15 Justice is a joy to the godly, but it causes dismay among evildoers.

16 The person who strays from common sense will end up in the company of the dead.

17 Those who love pleasure become poor; wine and luxury are not the way to riches.

18 Sometimes the wicked are punished to save the godly, and the treacherous for the upright.

19 It is better to live alone in the desert than with a crabby, complaining wife.

20 The wise have wealth and luxury, but fools spend whatever they get.

21 Whoever pursues godliness and unfailing love will find life, godliness, and honor.

22 The wise conquer the city of the strong and level the fortress in which they trust.

23 If you keep your mouth shut, you will stay out of trouble.

24 Mockers are proud and haughty; they act with boundless arrogance.

25 The desires of lazy people will be their ruin, for their hands refuse to work.

26 They are always greedy for more, while the godly love to give!

27 God loathes the sacrifice of an evil person, especially when it is brought with ulterior motives.

28 A false witness will be cut off, but an attentive witness will be allowed to speak.

29 The wicked put up a bold front, but the upright proceed with care.

30 Human plans, no matter how wise or well advised, cannot stand against the Lord.

31 The horses are prepared for battle, but the victory belongs to the Lord.

Questions for Reflection:

1. Make a list of what you consider important. What number is God on this list?

2. Specifically, name something God has asked you to do? How did you respond, with fear or faith?

3. Name several ways you can express your gratitude to the Lord.

Prayer:

I praise You, Lord, for every blessing You have granted me. Yet most of all, I love You for who You are – my Savior, my Lord, and my Provider.

– Secret 22 –
Mind Your Marriage

No other structure can replace the family.
Without it, our children have no moral foundation.
– Chuck Colson

A friend of mine was having serious family challenges and came to me for some advice one afternoon. Tom was very successful in his career and made a substantial income. Kind of a "man's man," he was a real outdoors person and an avid golfer.

During our conversation, I asked him, "Tom, how many hours have you spent on the golf course lately?"

He thought for a moment and answered, "Not my usual lately, because it's deer season and I've been gone almost every weekend. I just played 9 holes the other day after work."

Then I asked, "What about your golf lessons?"

"Oh," he quickly replied, "I'm still taking those on Tuesday mornings."

After a few more probes, finally, I asked a question that made him a little uneasy.

"Tom, what have you done to better educate yourself on the topics of marriage and family enrichment?"

Sheepishly and somewhat surprised, he answered, "Not any." And I replied, "Well, there you have it. I think I know why your marriage is headed for disaster."

Tom's family situation was in crisis for two main reasons:

1. He was not putting family on his high-priority list. He didn't understand the difference between quality *and* quantity time with them.
2. He failed to understand that personal relationships, marriage and parenting are much like any other skill worth mastering. They aren't learned by osmosis—you have to *study* and educate yourself about them.

The Book of Proverbs has much to offer concerning what it takes to have a rewarding family life. In previous chapters, we read and we know what valuable instruction the Lord gives us:

1. **We must learn to listen.** "Listen to your father's instruction. Pay attention and grow wise" (Proverbs 4:1).
2. **We must learn to forgive.** "Hatred stirs up quarrels, but love covers all offenses" (Proverbs 10:12).
3. **We must strive for peace.** "Those who bring trouble on their families inherit only the wind" (Proverbs 11:29).
4. **We must learn to keep our word.** "The Lord hates those who don't keep their word, but he delights in those who do" (Proverbs 12:22). (Don't misread this: He hates what is evil, but He always loves His children. He wants us to do what we say we'll do, to keep our word.)
5. **We must be a positive example and role model.** "The godly walk with integrity; blessed are their children after them" (Proverbs 20:7).

Today, Solomon shares the cardinal rule for avoiding catastrophe. This can apply to any situation (personal, family or career). He writes, "A prudent person foresees the danger ahead and takes precautions; the simpleton goes blindly on and suffers the consequences" (Proverbs 22:3).

I have to bring in the Apostle Paul again on this one, because he has such great advice in his letter to the Ephesians (chapter 5) about the family and "Spirit-guided" relationships:

21 And further, submit to one another out of reverence for Christ.

22 For wives, this means submit to your husbands as to the Lord.

23 For a husband is the head of his wife as Christ is the head of the church. He is the Savior of his body, the church.

24 As the church submits to Christ, so you wives should submit to your husbands in everything.

25 For husbands, this means love your wives, just as Christ loved the church. He gave up his life for her

26 to make her holy and clean, washed by the cleansing of God's word.

27 He did this to present her to himself as a glorious church without a spot or wrinkle or any other blemish. Instead, she will be holy and without fault.

28 In the same way, husbands ought to love their wives as they love their own bodies. For a man who loves his wife actually shows love for himself.

29 No one hates his own body but feeds and cares for it, just as Christ cares for the church.

30 And we are members of his body.

(Ephesians 5:21-30)–NLT

Have you spent time thinking, praying and studying about how to have better family relationships? In the process, you may find the heart of the problem is not your spouse or your children. It may be time for you to take a long hard look in the mirror. Before God can work in your family, He must first do a work in *you*.

Ask the Lord to give you the wisdom necessary to help you nurture and build a strong family life, or to make repairs to any damage done in the past, by asking for forgiveness. Many relationships have been restored because the one at fault simply asked the other members for forgiveness. It takes a humble person to ask, but the benefit is massive. Aside from our personal relationship to God, nothing is more important than marriage and family.

Let's make it a #1 priority to start minding our marriages, because "it takes two to *make* it, and one to *break* it."

Proverbs 22

1 Choose a good reputation over great riches, for being held in high esteem is better than having silver or gold.

2 The rich and the poor have this in common: The Lord made them both.

3 A prudent person foresees the danger ahead and takes precautions; the simpleton goes blindly on and suffers the consequences.

4 True humility and fear of the Lord lead to riches, honor, and long life.

5 The deceitful walk a thorny, treacherous road; whoever values life will stay away.

6 Teach your children to choose the right path, and when they are older, they will remain upon it.

7 Just as the rich rule the poor, so the borrower is servant to the lender.

8 Those who plant seeds of injustice will harvest disaster, and their reign of terror will end.

9 Blessed are those who are generous, because they feed the poor.

10 Throw out the mocker, and fighting, quarrels, and insults will disappear.

11 Anyone who loves a pure heart and gracious speech is the king's friend.

12 The Lord preserves knowledge, but he ruins the plans of the deceitful.

13 The lazy person is full of excuses, saying, "If I go outside, I might meet a lion in the street and be killed!"

14 The mouth of an immoral woman is a deep pit; those living under the Lord's displeasure will fall into it.

15 A youngster's heart is filled with foolishness, but discipline will drive it away.

16 A person who gets ahead by oppressing the poor or by showering gifts on the rich will end in poverty.

17 Listen to the words of the wise; apply your heart to my instruction.

18 For it is good to keep these sayings deep within yourself, always ready on your lips.

19 I am teaching you today—yes, you—so you will trust in the Lord.

20 I have written thirty sayings for you, filled with advice and knowledge.

21 In this way, you may know the truth and bring an accurate report to those who sent you.

22 Do not rob the poor because they are poor or exploit the needy in court.

23 For the Lord is their defender. He will injure anyone who injures them.

24 Keep away from angry, short-tempered people,

25 or you will learn to be like them and endanger your soul.

26 Do not co-sign another person's note or put up a guarantee for someone else's loan.

27 If you can't pay it, even your bed will be snatched from under you.

28 Do not steal your neighbor's property by moving the ancient boundary markers set up by your ancestors.

29 Do you see any truly competent workers? They will serve kings rather than ordinary people.

Questions for Reflection:

1. If there were one thing you could change about your family situation, what would it be? What can be let go? What should you hang on to?

2. How could you be a better example in your home?

3. Have you done any research lately about how to improve your current situation? (e.g., books, audio CDs, videos or seminars?)

4. What is God's desire for your family?

Prayer:

Father, please give me the wisdom and knowledge to bring my family closer to each other—and to You. Help me to demonstrate the unconditional love, acceptance and forgiveness You expect of me.

– Secret 23 –
Chop the Chains

Freedom is the oxygen of the soul.
– Moshe Dayan

Do you ever experience these frustrations?

- I feel helpless
- Things will never change for me
- My world is caving in
- I'm a hostage to my circumstances
- Why does this always happen to me?
- If I could find the right job, I'd be happy
- If I were married, it would be like heaven
- If I were divorced, life would be much better
- Where is God when I need Him?

Did you notice that most of the above attitudes and feelings include personal pronouns (I, me and my). In other words, the attention is focused on SELF! It's OK to thing about ourselves and our needs from time to time, but we have to be careful about being so self-absorbed to the point that "me" is all we see. Self-focus is a guarantee for frustration.

Of course, we all get frustrated from time to time. It's just a part of the human life cycle. Though other people play a part in our frustrations, if we're honest, we'll have to admit that we tend to bring a lot of these situations on ourselves. As I've said before, it's all in *how* we respond.

We also must realize that our response (positive or negative) is not an "inherited trait," but something we actually *learn*—with a ton of repetition to reinforce it.

Ivan Pavlov, a Russian scientist, coined the phrase "Classical Conditioning" or "stimulus-response." Do you recall the test Pavlov performed with the dog, and every time the bell rang, food would drop in the bowl? After a few times, he noticed that just by hearing the bell, the canine would salivate even when there was no food present. In fact, it got to the point that when the dog would just hear the scientist walk into the room, he would begin salivating.

We humans get conditioned in a similar way.

If we continually respond in the same fashion to our stimuli, we become programmed to repeat that behavior. Then it becomes habit and much more difficult to break free.

Let's carry that thought one step further. If we can be conditioned to react in a *negative* way, we can also learn to respond in a *positive* manner. We don't have to remain trapped without help or hope!

A great object lesson in conditioning can be found in the behavior of the Indian elephant—a huge animal that can weigh as much as five tons. These creatures are often domesticated very early in life and trained to be docile and easily controlled by their owners.

The way they accomplish this feat is rather simple. When the elephant is a baby, the owner chains it to a large stake driven deeply into the ground. The elephant flays and struggles against the restraint hour after hour. Finally, exhausted, it gives up and accepts the fact that when it is tethered, it's helpless—and it is useless to attempt an escape.

For the rest of the elephant's life, all the owner needs to do is tie a thin rope around the animal's leg and attach it to a small stick in the ground in order to "hold" the elephant securely. The moment the animal just feels the rope, it stops struggling.

The elephant has *learned* to be helpless. And even though it could easily escape, it no longer strains against the leash. The giant animal may have the ability and strength to knock down houses, but it remains captive and easily controlled because of its prior conditioning.

Like that elephant, we allow ourselves to think of the reasons WHY NOT to try something, rather than the reasons WHY or HOW it CAN be done.

Think for a moment: What is your "stick in the ground?"

- A parent (or yourself) telling you you'll never amount to anything?
- School mates taunting you?
- A physical flaw or handicap?
- Cruel, demeaning words from a relative?
- Your boss telling you that you don't have what it takes to succeed?

Let's change that thought process! Start concentrating on **how we can** achieve something great; not on **why we can't**. Let's channel our energies in the direction of accomplishment, rather than toward failure and frustration.

Listen to these words: "For surely you have a future ahead of you; your hope will not be disappointed" (Proverbs 23:18). Is your thinking that of a "victim" or "victor?" The letters "im" instead of the "or" make a huge difference in the outcome. Notice that the victim's focus is on the IM, the "I'm" (personal pronoun).

Perhaps something has you in a stranglehold, but is actually anchored to something trivial. What steps can you take to break free and reach your potential?

God didn't send His Son to earth to keep you in bondage. Jesus came to break the chains and give you ultimate liberty. The Lord Himself said in John 8:44, "You shall know the truth, and the truth shall set you free." Since Jesus is the *truth*, when you come to know Him personally, He wakes up that greatness, that potential that He Himself put inside you the day you trusted Him as your Savior.

The Apostle Paul said, "Christ has really set us free. Now make sure that you stay free" (Galatians 5:1). And again he reminds us, "I can do all things through Christ who gives me strength" (Philippians 4:13).

The decision is up to you. With the Lord's help, yank that rope and cut those chains of inadequacy!

Proverbs 23

1 When dining with a ruler, pay attention to what is put before you.

2 If you are a big eater, put a knife to your throat,

3 and don't desire all the delicacies—deception may be involved.

4 Don't weary yourself trying to get rich. Why waste your time?

5 For riches can disappear as though they had the wings of a bird!

6 Don't eat with people who are stingy; don't desire their delicacies.

7 "Eat and drink," they say, but they don't mean it. They are always thinking about how much it costs.

8 You will vomit up the delicious food they serve, and you will have to take back your words of appreciation for their "kindness."

9 Don't waste your breath on fools, for they will despise the wisest advice.

10 Don't steal the land of defenseless orphans by moving the ancient boundary markers,

11 for their Redeemer is strong. He himself will bring their charges against you.

12 Commit yourself to instruction; attune your ears to hear words of knowledge.

13 Don't fail to correct your children. They won't die if you spank them.

14 Physical discipline may well save them from death.

15 My child, how I will rejoice if you become wise.

16 Yes, my heart will thrill when you speak what is right and just.

17 Don't envy sinners, but always continue to fear the Lord.

18 For surely you have a future ahead of you; your hope will not be disappointed.

19 My child, listen and be wise. Keep your heart on the right course.

20 Do not carouse with drunkards and gluttons,

21 for they are on their way to poverty. Too much sleep clothes a person with rags.

22 Listen to your father, who gave you life, and don't despise your mother's experience when she is old.

23 Get the truth and don't ever sell it; also get wisdom, discipline, and discernment.

24 The father of godly children has cause for joy. What a pleasure it is to have wise children.

25 So give your parents joy! May she who gave you birth be happy.

26 O my son, give me your heart. May your eyes delight in my ways of wisdom.

27 A prostitute is a deep pit; an adulterous woman is treacherous.

28 She hides and waits like a robber, looking for another victim who will be unfaithful to his wife.

29 Who has anguish? Who has sorrow? Who is always fighting? Who is always complaining? Who has unnecessary bruises? Who has bloodshot eyes?

30 It is the one who spends long hours in the taverns, trying out new drinks.

31 Don't let the sparkle and smooth taste of wine deceive you.

32 For in the end it bites like a poisonous serpent; it stings like a viper.

33 You will see hallucinations, and you will say crazy things.

34 You will stagger like a sailor tossed at sea, clinging to a swaying mast.

35 And you will say, "They hit me, but I didn't feel it. I didn't even know it when they beat me up. When will I wake up so I can have another drink?"

Questions for Reflection:

1. Name three goals or dreams you've never followed through on because you thought you would fail.

2. How has Christ's gift of freedom made a difference in your life? Are you applying that freedom?

3. What are some ways you can encourage others who feel helpless and hopeless?

Prayer:

Lord, I know that You are the source of my freedom. Help me to focus on Your power and not on my fears and limitations. Give me the courage to take my foot off the brake when you want me to press on.

– Secret 24 –
Adhere Adversity

Failure is delay, but not defeat.
It is a temporary detour, not a dead-end street.
– William Arthur Ward

Failure has been called the foundation of success. It's true. Without mistakes and setbacks we can never fully understand or appreciate a victory.

Jack Canfield and Mark Victor Hansen, in their book, *A 3rd Serving of Chicken Soup for the Soul*, include the account of how Thomas Edison's laboratory in West Orange, New Jersey, was virtually destroyed by fire in December 1914.

Although the damage exceeded $2 million, the buildings were only insured for $238,000 because they were made of concrete and thought to be fireproof. Much of Edison's life's work went up in spectacular flames that December night.

At the height of the fire, Edison's 24-year old son, Charles, frantically searched for his father among the smoke and debris. He finally found him, calmly watching the scene, his face glowing in the reflection, his white hair blowing in the wind.

"My heart ached for him," said Charles. "He was 67—no longer a young man—and everything was going up in flames. When he saw me, he shouted, 'Charles, where's your mother?' When I told him I didn't know, he said, 'Find her. Bring her here. She will never see anything like this as long as she lives.'"

The next morning, Edison looked at the ruins and said, "There is great value in disaster. All our mistakes are burned up. Thank God we can start anew."

Three weeks after the fire, Edison managed to deliver his first phonograph. Just because you're down, doesn't mean you're defeated!

Proverbs tell us: "They may trip seven times, but each time they will rise again" (Proverbs 24:16).

Chuck Colson, former Special Counsel to the President, was the first member of the Nixon administration to be sent to prison for Watergate-related charges. During those dark days, Colson had a life-altering experience with Jesus Christ and up to the time of his death was a highly respected Christian author and radio personality.

Looking back on the past, Colson recalled, "When the frustration of my helplessness seemed greatest, I discovered God's grace was more than sufficient. After my imprisonment, I could look back and see how God used my powerlessness for His purpose." And he added, "What He has chosen for my most significant witness was not my triumphs or victories, but my defeat." What's the lesson? When dark clouds cover your life and you can't seem to find a ray of sunshine, just remember, there is still hope in God through Jesus Christ.

Solomon's advice to us is to stop trying to solve our problems alone, but to seek God's help and wisdom. He says, "...wisdom is sweet to your soul. If you find it, you will have a bright future, and your hopes will not be cut short" (Proverbs 24:14). Jesus tells us in the Gospel of John that we have the Holy Spirit living inside of us, and we are never alone—EVER! (See John 14-16).

The next time your battery needs a quick recharge, read the words of Paul to the believers at Corinth: "We are pressed on every side by troubles, but we are not crushed and broken. We are perplexed, but we don't give up and quit. We are hunted down, but God never abandons us. We get knocked down, but we get up again and keep going" (2 Corinthians 4:8-9).

Adhere to adversity. Victory follows defeat!

Proverbs 24

1 Don't envy evil people; don't desire their company.

2 For they spend their days plotting violence, and their words are always stirring up trouble.

3 A house is built by wisdom and becomes strong through good sense.

4 Through knowledge its rooms are filled with all sorts of precious riches and valuables.

5 A wise man is mightier than a strong man, and a man of knowledge is more powerful than a strong man.

6 So don't go to war without wise guidance; victory depends on having many counselors.

7 Wisdom is too much for a fool. When the leaders gather, the fool has nothing to say.

8 A person who plans evil will get a reputation as a troublemaker.

9 The schemes of a fool are sinful; everyone despises a mocker.

10 If you fail under pressure, your strength is not very great.

11 Rescue those who are unjustly sentenced to death; don't stand back and let them die.

12 Don't try to avoid responsibility by saying you didn't know about it. For God knows all hearts, and he sees you. He keeps watch over your soul, and he knows you knew! And he will judge all people according to what they have done.

13 My child, eat honey, for it is good, and the honeycomb is sweet to the taste.

14 In the same way, wisdom is sweet to your soul. If you find it, you will have a bright future, and your hopes will not be cut short.

15 Do not lie in wait like an outlaw at the home of the godly. And don't raid the house where the godly live.

16 They may trip seven times, but each time they will rise again. But one calamity is enough to lay the wicked low.

17 Do not rejoice when your enemies fall into trouble. Don't be happy when they stumble.

18 For the Lord will be displeased with you and will turn his anger away from them.

19 Do not fret because of evildoers; don't envy the wicked.

20 For the evil have no future; their light will be snuffed out.

21 My child, fear the Lord and the king, and don't associate with rebels.

22 For you will go down with them to sudden disaster. Who knows where the punishment from the Lord and the king will end?

23 Here are some further sayings of the wise: It is wrong to show favoritism when passing judgment.

24 A judge who says to the wicked, "You are innocent," will be cursed by many people and denounced by the nations.

25 But blessings are showered on those who convict the guilty.

26 It is an honor to receive an honest reply.

27 Develop your business first before building your house.

28 Do not testify spitefully against innocent neighbors; don't lie about them.

29 And don't say, "Now I can pay them back for all their meanness to me! I'll get even!"

30 I walked by the field of a lazy person, the vineyard of one lacking sense.

31 I saw that it was overgrown with thorns. It was covered with weeds, and its walls were broken down.

32 Then, as I looked and thought about it, I learned this lesson:

33 A little extra sleep, a little more slumber, a little folding of the hands to rest—

34 and poverty will pounce on you like a bandit; scarcity will attack you like an armed robber.

Questions for Reflection:

1. Can you think of an unfortunate circumstance that came your way which was actually a blessing in disguise?
2. Why do bad things happen to good people?
3. In what ways do problems make us stronger?

Prayer:

Lord, in this world, difficulties arise and bad things happen. Help me to seek the good in every situation and recognize that Your hand is at work in my life—making me stronger by the minute.

– Secret 25 –
Handle Habits

Habit is a cable. We weave a thread of it every day
until it becomes so strong we cannot break it.
–Horace Mann

When I was a kid, my dad would take me with him to the gas station with him to get the car serviced. He used to call it a "lube job."

The mechanic would elevate the car on one of those hydraulic rack contraptions, and I distinctly remember him walking under the car with a grease gun, connecting the end of the tube to each zerk (grease fitting) to replenish the grease.

Thinking back, here's what fascinated me the most about this: Not once did the mechanic ever attempt to scoop and scrape all the old grease out of those tough-to-get places—that would have been impossible.

Instead, when he attached the hose to the zerk, he'd pump the new grease into the pocket. As a result, the old, black, used-up grease was forced out of the crevasse, falling to the concrete floor, then scooped up and thrown away.

In with the good, out with the bad.

Research in human behavior has concluded that the most effective way to eliminate a bad habit is NOT to attempt to "get rid" of the habit, but rather, "replace it" with a *good* one. Some call this the "Principle of Substitution," substituting one habit for the other.

Any parent of a toddler should know about this handy technique. Aside from a life-and-death situation, it's not always the best idea to take the slobbery dog toy away from your child without giving him (or her) something better in return to play with. This strategy redirects the child's focus and attention from what the parent took away to what he was given in its place (and it could save your hearing from all the screaming).

Alcoholics Anonymous has had tremendous success in helping people break the cycle of addictive drinking. One of their secrets is requiring regular attendance at their meetings, instead of hanging out in the neighborhood bar. In other words, it's a "positive exchange."

At some point we must make the decision to grow up and take charge our lives; and one way to do this is to exercise self-control with our habits.

Today's chapter of Proverbs ends with these words: "A person without self-control is as defenseless as a city with broken-down walls" (Proverbs 25:28). This is not the place you want to be.

In Old Testament times, a city without walls was a sure-fire target for invasion. The inhabitants were defenseless. That's how it is for those lacking self-control—they're at the mercy of their emotions and cravings. Then, before long, they fall prey to life-destroying patterns and addictions.

So how do you handle a bad habit? Believe it or not, It's a three step process:

1. **REALIZE**—Admit the habit—Own up to the fact you have an undesirable habit. Tell the Lord about it (He already knows anyway; it helps you to open up with Him about it).

2. **REPLACE**—Trade the bad behavior for something better, as I stated earlier. Instead of saying, "I'm going to stop smoking," replace it with, "I only breathe clean, fresh air." Instead of announcing "I'm out of shape," say, "I'm feeling better now that I'm beginning my new walking program." Once again, it's all about where you focus. What you *think* about, *dominates* you.

3. **REPEAT**—Not only stick with the new habit, but be diligent and persistent through repetition! Every day will bring you closer to forming and solidifying your new habit. And when you force yourself to practice the new behavior, even though you don't "feel" like doing it, you'll be "adding one more strand to the cord"; and before long, you'll have a rope!

Did you know, according to some researchers, it takes anywhere from 21-30 days to establish any habit (good or bad)? And, no, it's not very much fun since there's a lot of "push" involved in creating the new and discarding the old. But the effort is well worth it.

In a previous chapter, I mentioned a space rocket blasting off. The rocket must keep pushing—lifting off—to free itself from the earth's gravitational pull. The key for us is to keep "pushing" forward with our new habits until we experience the release, the freedom; then we can "ease back on the engines." Before long, we begin to experience the new habits developing, and they soon become more automatic, second nature.

Remember, we're not in these struggles by ourselves. A key verse of hope for us is: "For I can do everything through Christ, who gives me strength" (Philippians 4:13).

Decide today to give up trying to eliminate old, bad habits and refocus your attention toward developing new ones. Then you'll be able to say, "...the old life is gone. A new life has begun!" (2 Corinthians 5:17).

Let's pray for each other so we can better handle our habits—especially the GOOD ones!

Proverbs 25

1 These are more proverbs of Solomon, collected by the advisers of King Hezekiah of Judah.

2 It is God's privilege to conceal things and the king's privilege to discover them.

3 No one can discover the height of heaven, the depth of the earth, or all that goes on in the king's mind!

4 Remove the dross from silver, and the sterling will be ready for the silversmith. 5 Remove the wicked from the king's court, and his reign will be made secure by justice.

6 Don't demand an audience with the king or push for a place among the great.

7 It is better to wait for an invitation than to be sent to the end of the line, publicly disgraced! Just because you see something,

8 don't be in a hurry to go to court. You might go down before your neighbors in shameful defeat.

9 So discuss the matter with them privately. Don't tell anyone else,

10 or others may accuse you of gossip. Then you will never regain your good reputation.

11 Timely advice is as lovely as golden apples in a silver basket.

12 Valid criticism is as treasured by the one who heeds it as jewelry made from finest gold.

13 Faithful messengers are as refreshing as snow in the heat of summer. They revive the spirit of their employer.

14 A person who doesn't give a promised gift is like clouds and wind that don't bring rain.

15 Patience can persuade a prince, and soft speech can crush strong opposition.

16 Do you like honey? Don't eat too much of it, or it will make you sick!

17 Don't visit your neighbors too often, or you will wear out your welcome.

18 Telling lies about others is as harmful as hitting them with an ax, wounding them with a sword, or shooting them with a sharp arrow.

19 Putting confidence in an unreliable person is like chewing with a toothache or walking on a broken foot.

20 Singing cheerful songs to a person whose heart is heavy is as bad as stealing someone's jacket in cold weather or rubbing salt in a wound.

21 If your enemies are hungry, give them food to eat. If they are thirsty, give them water to drink.

22 You will heap burning coals on their heads, and the Lord will reward you.

23 As surely as a wind from the north brings rain, so a gossiping tongue causes anger!

24 It is better to live alone in the corner of an attic than with a contentious wife in a lovely home.

25 Good news from far away is like cold water to the thirsty.

26 If the godly compromise with the wicked, it is like polluting a fountain or muddying a spring.

27 Just as it is not good to eat too much honey, it is not good for people to think about all the honors they deserve.

28 A person without self-control is as defenseless as a city with broken-down walls.

Questions for Reflection:

1. Identify two or three undesirable habits you'd like to replace (remember: habits can also be attitudes).
2. What new habits can you use as replacements?
3. How are your habits (good or bad) affecting your reputation and relationships?
4. How many spiritual habits are you working on (e.g., Bible study, meditation, etc.)?

Prayer:

Dear God, I ask You to be the Lord of my desires and habits. Please help me control my impulses, knowing I can do all things because You strengthen me. Give me the desire to replace the old with the new. Thanks for the push!

– Secret 26 –
Love Thy Labor

If a man is called to be a street sweeper, he should sweep streets even as Michelangelo painted, or Beethoven composed music or Shakespeare wrote poetry. He should sweep streets so well that all the hosts of heaven and earth will pause to say, here lived a great street sweeper who did his job well.
– Martin Luther King, Jr.

The former host of the "Tonight Show," the late Johnny Carson, once said, "Never continue in a job you don't enjoy. If you're happy in what you're doing, you'll like yourself, you will have inner peace. And if you have that, along with physical health, you will have had more success than you could possibly have imagined."

Do you enjoy your current job? If your answer is "yes," I'll bet you're in the minority. Most people don't enjoy their occupations.

Based on the conversations I've had with many folks, I would speculate that 85% would change jobs right away if they felt they could move into work with which they had a passion. And that's the key—having PASSION, doing something they love and care about. But most people feel that this "passion work" is out of reach for them. So they keep plodding along, doing what they don't like, every day, year-in and year-out.

It's not known who came up with this definition of insanity—which I'm sure you've heard many times—but it's still true just the same: "Insanity is doing the *same thing* over and over again and expecting a *different result*." We can become like the hamster in the spinning wheel. But our work doesn't have to be this way.

Before you make your next career move, spend some time by yourself with the Lord, and talk to Him about it. As you're praying, have a pen and pad of paper handy. Making a list, ask God to show you what you're good at, gifted for, and would really like to do. Jot down your strengths and talents, and then ask God to show you any opportunities that allow you to express your abilities. And if you can't find the career you want, maybe God might be telling you to start something, to blaze a new trail.

Here's more great advice from inspirational speaker, Denis Waitley: "Chase your passion, not your pension." In other words, do something you love, and don't just do it for the money.

Unfortunately, most people look at the money first. I've met some fairly well-off people who are pretty miserable—not because of their income, but because they don't care for their job situation!

If you're in a job or career situation you abhor, I don't think you should blame the company for your dissatisfaction, especially if you don't enjoy being there in the first place. You were created by God with the gift of choice. No one put a gun to your head and said, "You'd better take this job, or else!" As I said in the Introduction, we are responsible! You and I are responsible for everything we do.

Now if you're in a situation where you *do* like your job, but aren't making enough money, listen to what sales trainer and motivational speaker, Brian Tracy, says: "If you would like a pay raise, just go to the nearest mirror, negotiate with your boss [you], and your raise will become effective when *you* do!" Now that might mean getting a different job somewhere else, or taking on a second job, but regardless, *you* are the President of You, Inc. You are responsible for your pay raises, even if you have to sell something on eBay or have a garage sale.

I'm not trying to sound cold or hard, but I want to encourage you to move forward and begin the transition of doing something you truly love—even if it means temporarily earning less money. This temporary job situation won't last forever, and you could treat it as "transitional work" on the way to something you really would like to do. The key is to not lose sight of the work you desire, and keep searching for that great opportunity.

When you're passionate about your job, you'll be amazed at your productivity, as well as your motivation. A friend once told me, "I can't believe I'm actually getting paid for doing what I love! I don't feel like I go to work; I feel like every day I go to play."

Here's a good way to look at "job." A job is nothing more than "solving a problem or concern" for someone else. That's it. That's all a job is—*solving problems!* So, a good starting place might be *not* to look for a job, but search for a *problem* to solve. *You* become your clients' *answer* or *solution* to their situation! This should be your focus in a job interview. The potential employer will look at you in a totally different light if you approach work in this manner. Nobody really wants to hire employees; they prefer "problem solvers."

You know as well as I do, there are boat loads of problems out there that people need help with. You just might be their new solution! Regarding my work and ministry, I approach it this way: I look for churches and companies who have a "laughter or humor deficiency." They need their employees or church members to lighten up a little. Well, *I* am their guy! *I* am the one who can *solve that problem.* And I also give them an extra bonus: ministry, motivation and inspiration.

Have you ever noticed that most folks who love their work rarely experience lengthy times of low motivation or laziness? They seem to have a continual enthusiasm for what they're doing.

In Proverbs we are told: "Work hard and become a leader; be lazy and become a slave" (Proverbs 12:24). We also find, "As a door turns back and forth on its hinges, so the lazy person turns over in bed" (Proverbs 26:14). Talk about lack of motivation!

Andrew Carnegie observed, "The average person puts only 25 percent of his energy and ability into his work. The world takes off its hat to those who put in more than 50 percent of their capacity, and stands on its head for those few-and-far-between souls who devote 100 percent."

Work is a gift from God—a treasure to enjoy. That's why I believe life is far too short for us to be permanently employed in a situation in which we aren't happy and fulfilled most of the time, especially in America.

Does this mean all work—even the kind you love—won't at times be drudgery? Absolutely not! We all have good and bad days at work. But I'm convinced it's better to have consistently wonderful, satisfying work with a few negative periods here and there, than to have a career you despise with only a few good days scattered throughout.

Regarding career paths, I believe that God leads us in the direction of our gifts and talents He's implanted within us. If you can't stomach numbers, you probably shouldn't be an accountant. If you have to work too hard to stay on pitch, you just may not be cut out for a singing career. On the other hand, you might enjoy working on cars, teaching history, or making people laugh. The key is to find *your* inclinations and strengths, then go to work on them.

Many have a problem understanding the difference between "purpose" and "calling." Let me explain.

As followers of Christ, we all should have the same purpose—that is, to glorify and honor the Lord. Our "calling" is how we go about fulfilling and living out God's purpose with our work. You and I can have many different callings (i.e., jobs, careers) throughout our lifetimes. In this day and age, careers change frequently. But a Christian's purpose never changes— we are to always glorify God in everything we do.

We need to be willing and courageous enough to take steps in the direction God is leading us. Pray and ask Him for direction concerning your life's occupation. You don't have to be too concerned about getting "off track," as I mentioned earlier. Remember, God will find you and nudge you back.

Fear is one of the biggest challenges we face, because the last thing we want to do is fail! We all fear failure to some degree. But the key to victory is to keep the fear from paralyzing us. Here's a great acrostic for "F-E-A-R":

False
Evidence
Appearing
Real

WOW! False Evidence *Appearing* Real! It's the "appearing" part that gets us. But we can't focus on the appearance of something that is not really there. Let that vision go! See it for what it really is—false evidence!

We don't know our futures anyway, only God knows. So we really don't have anything to lose. But we have everything to gain because God is *with* us and *in* us. We simply need to move forward and know that He'll give us course-correction as we need it.

Here's a promise you can take to the bank: "Commit your work to the Lord, and then your plans will succeed." (Proverbs 16:3).

Find out what your strengths are, and then make every effort to "love thy labor" for the glory of God.

Proverbs 26

1 Honor doesn't go with fools any more than snow with summer or rain with harvest.

2 Like a fluttering sparrow or a darting swallow, an unfair curse will not land on its intended victim.

3 Guide a horse with a whip, a donkey with a bridle, and a fool with a rod to his back!

4 When arguing with fools, don't answer their foolish arguments, or you will become as foolish as they are.

5 When arguing with fools, be sure to answer their foolish arguments, or they will become wise in their own estimation.

6 Trusting a fool to convey a message is as foolish as cutting off one's feet or drinking poison!

7 In the mouth of a fool, a proverb becomes as limp as a paralyzed leg.

8 Honoring a fool is as foolish as tying a stone to a slingshot.

9 A proverb in a fool's mouth is as dangerous as a thornbush brandished by a drunkard.

10 An employer who hires a fool or a bystander is like an archer who shoots recklessly.

11 As a dog returns to its vomit, so a fool repeats his folly.

12 There is more hope for fools than for people who think they are wise.

13 The lazy person is full of excuses, saying, "I can't go outside because there might be a lion on the road! Yes, I'm sure there's a lion out there!"

14 As a door turns back and forth on its hinges, so the lazy person turns over in bed.

15 Some people are so lazy that they won't lift a finger to feed themselves.

16 Lazy people consider themselves smarter than seven wise counselors.

17 Yanking a dog's ears is as foolish as interfering in someone else's argument.

18 Just as damaging as a mad man shooting a lethal weapon

19 is someone who lies to a friend and then says, "I was only joking."

20 Fire goes out for lack of fuel, and quarrels disappear when gossip stops.

21 A quarrelsome person starts fights as easily as hot embers light charcoal or fire lights wood.

22 What dainty morsels rumors are—but they sink deep into one's heart.

23 Smooth words may hide a wicked heart, just as a pretty glaze covers a common clay pot.

24 People with hate in their hearts may sound pleasant enough, but don't believe them.

25 Though they pretend to be kind, their hearts are full of all kinds of evil.

26 While their hatred may be concealed by trickery, it will finally come to light for all to see.

27 If you set a trap for others, you will get caught in it yourself. If you roll a boulder down on others, it will roll back and crush you.

28 A lying tongue hates its victims, and flattery causes ruin.

Questions for Reflection:

1. If anything were possible, what would you change about your job or career?

2. What are your natural-born strengths? Make a list of these.

3. What three steps can you take to make your current employment situation more enjoyable?

4. What do you sense the Lord is telling you concerning your future work? Is your number one priority to follow His advice?

Prayer:

Lord, I commit my gifts, talents and the labor of my hands to You. Through the opportunities You have given, may I honor You, provide for my family and serve others today.

– Secret 27 –
Watch Your Words

Little keys can open big locks. Simple words can express great thoughts. – William Arthur Ward

Susan had a serious problem with gossip. She repeated a juicy tale about a neighbor, only to learn later it was untrue.

Within a few days the whole community knew the story. The neighbor was deeply hurt and offended. Susan was mortified and went to her minister to find out what she could do to repair the damage.

He advised, "Go and purchase a feather pillow. Cut it open, then, on your way home, scatter the feathers one by one along the road. Then come back to see me tomorrow." Although Susan was slightly puzzled, she followed his instructions exactly.

The next day the minister gave her new instructions: "Now, go and collect all those feathers you dropped yesterday and bring them back to me."

Susan replied, "You know I can't do that! Those feathers are long gone by now."

"You see," said the minister, "it's easy to drop them, but it is impossible to get them all back. That's how it is with your words." Words are powerful, both written and spoken.

Recently, I noticed a bumper sticker on the back of an old beat-up car with some demeaning words that read: "People Suck!" I thought *who dumped on this guy to make him so bitter? With that mindset,* no wonder *he was driving that piece of junk! He must have forgotten that "people" made that car!*

Also, with that attitude, would you ever consider hiring this guy? Would you want him to date your daughter? Would you invite this "Mr. Attitude" guy to a career workshop? Obviously, this fellow didn't understand the power of words and the kind of damage they can bring about. I can tell you, that guy's future was being determined by the words he displayed, even if only through a bumper sticker.

I'll never forget these words I once read before, but can't find the source: "Be careful of the words you say, keep them soft and sweet; you never know from day to day which ones you're going to eat!"

A common thread throughout the Book of Proverbs concerns the words we speak. The Life Application Bible mentions four types of tongues:

1. The controlled tongue: "Don't talk too much, for it fosters sin. Be sensible and turn off the flow!" (Proverbs 10:19).

2. The caring tongue: "The godly speak words that are helpful, but the wicked speak only what is corrupt" (Proverbs 10:32).

3. The conniving tongue: "Here is a description of worthless and wicked people: They are constant liars, signaling their true intentions to their friends by making signs with their eyes and feet and fingers. Their perverted hearts plot evil. They stir up trouble constantly" (Proverbs 6:12-14).

4. The careless tongue: "Some people make cutting remarks, but the words of the wise bring healing" (Proverbs 12:18).

Today's reading in Proverbs begins with a warning about using words to boast or heap praise upon oneself. Solomon advises, "Don't brag about tomorrow, since you don't know what the day will bring. Don't praise yourself; let others do it" (Proverbs 27:1-2). In other words, praise sounds much better coming from someone else's mouth than your own.

The reason Solomon instructs his readers to guard what they say is because words can bring life or death—depending on how they're used. I once heard the great concluding line from the poem, *The First Settlers Story* by Will Carleton: "Thoughts unexpressed may sometimes fall back dead; but God Himself can't kill them once they're said."

Let's practice better word watching, because words are extremely powerful—for good or evil. Choose and use words that benefit others and honor the Lord.

You might want to watch your words and treat them like those feathers!

Proverbs 27

1 Don't brag about tomorrow, since you don't know what the day will bring.

2 Don't praise yourself; let others do it!

3 A stone is heavy and sand is weighty, but the resentment caused by a fool is heavier than both.

4 Anger is cruel, and wrath is like a flood, but who can survive the destructiveness of jealousy?

5 An open rebuke is better than hidden love!

6 Wounds from a friend are better than many kisses from an enemy.

7 Honey seems tasteless to a person who is full, but even bitter food tastes sweet to the hungry.

8 A person who strays from home is like a bird that strays from its nest.

9 The heartfelt counsel of a friend is as sweet as perfume and incense.

10 Never abandon a friend – either yours or your father's. Then in your time of need, you won't have to ask your relatives for assistance. It is better to go to a neighbor than to a relative who lives far away.

11 My child, how happy I will be if you turn out to be wise! Then I will be able to answer my critics.

12 A prudent person foresees the danger ahead and takes precautions. The simpleton goes blindly on and suffers the consequences.

13 Be sure to get collateral from anyone who guarantees the debt of a stranger. Get a deposit if someone guarantees the debt of an adulterous woman.

14 If you shout a pleasant greeting to your neighbor too early in the morning, it will be counted as a curse!

15 A nagging wife is as annoying as the constant dripping on a rainy day.

16 Trying to stop her complaints is like trying to stop the wind or hold something with greased hands.

17 As iron sharpens iron, a friend sharpens a friend.

18 Workers who tend a fig tree are allowed to eat its fruit. In the same way, workers who protect their employer's interests will be rewarded.

19 As a face is reflected in water, so the heart reflects the person.

20 Just as Death and Destruction are never satisfied, so human desire is never satisfied.

21 Fire tests the purity of silver and gold, but a person is tested by being praised.

22 You cannot separate fools from their foolishness, even though you grind them like grain with mortar and pestle.

23 Know the state of your flocks, and put your heart into caring for your herds,

24 for riches don't last forever, and the crown might not be secure for the next generation.

25 After the hay is harvested, the new crop appears, and the mountain grasses are gathered in,

26 your sheep will provide wool for clothing, and your goats will be sold for the price of a field.

27 And you will have enough goats' milk for you, your family, and your servants.

Questions for Reflection:

1. Are there any aspects of your vocabulary you need to improve? Do you come across negatively or positively to those you interact with?

2. Since you are known by the words you speak, would you say that your words enhance or hinder your reputation?

3. Is there someone you owe an apology for something hurtful you said to them?

4. Would you agree that the Holy Spirit has control of your communication?

Prayer:

Lord, teach me when to speak and when to remain silent. Make me aware of the destructive force of words. Help my speech to build, not to tear down Your Kingdom.

– Secret 28 –
Seek Serenity

Calm self-confidence is as far from conceit as the desire to earn a decent living is remote from greed.
– Channing Pollock

We live in a troubled world. There is chaos everywhere we turn. And it's very difficult to get away from, since Cable News, newspapers, Smart Phones, Tablets and other avenues of media continually slap us in the face instantaneously. But we shouldn't be surprised by this, because Christ said that this would be the case—in this world we will have trouble (see John 16:33).

Since our earthly existence is chaotic—and it's not going to get any better—how do we handle the turmoil?

Well we can't just stop chaos, but we can decide how we let it affect us. The great news for us as followers of Christ is that we can have peace and serenity in the midst of difficulty, much like being in the "eye" of a hurricane. Peace and calmness are only in the center, and that's where our focus should be when trouble surrounds us.

I cannot describe this subject of calmness much better than the late Earl Nightingale from his audio program *The Essence of Success*. So I'm going to let him tell you:

In a world filled with trouble and terror, those who radiate quiet composure seem odd and rare. People who stay cool, calm and collected are often viewed as "not in touch with the real world." What gives an individual the ability to remain in control in life's trying moments? The secret to serenity is not what is seen on the surface, but what lies deep inside.

Have you ever been at sea when a storm is brewing? As troubling as it may seem to you, there's much more to consider. Two or three hundred feet below the ocean it is calm and tranquil—and the fish at that depth don't notice the weather. Don't give outside forces permission to dictate your attitude or emotions. The headlines shouldn't determine whether you have a good or bad day. You make that choice!

Perhaps you've seen a grey heron. The heron is a tall, lanky bird with a long neck, a heavy dagger-shaped bill and a wing span of about six feet. These birds demonstrate an effective way to respond in the midst of trouble. They are extremely patient, often standing still for hours stalking their prey when they're on the offensive. But when the heron is pursued by an eagle, its number one enemy, it does not fly away in a panic. Instead, it remains calm and faces the enemy head-on.

Finally, the hungry eagle makes the strike, and to its surprise, the eagle is often pierced and badly injured by the sharp, spear-like bill of the quiet heron. It's a little too late, but I'm sure the eagle wishes he would have chosen a different opponent!

Here are a couple of life lessons I hope we can learn from this scenario:

1. **Remain calm during a crisis**—When we are confronted by unfavorable circumstances, people, difficulty and trials, it's best to not panic, but *remain calm*. We can think more clearly when we stay calm, and the end result can be wiser decisions.
2. **Problems can solve themselves**—Many times the problems or situations that attempt to pounce upon us often have a way of

dissolving or turning back on themselves, much like the eagle impaling himself on the heron.

It's wise to remain calm as much as possible in tense situations, especially if you're in conflict with a family member or a friend. Stay calm and cool. Seek serenity. Remember, "A hothead starts fights; a cool-tempered person tries to stop them" (Proverbs 15:18). A cool-tempered person is one who chooses to be calm and relaxed.

Fighting back or retaliating when we're attacked is similar to pouring gasoline on a fire to put it out. Sure, the gas is wet (i.e., it seems effective) but it's the wrong stuff and it doesn't work. The "water" of calmness is much more effective.

Never respond or react too soon. I have discovered that when our dogs track mud on the carpet, the first thing I want to do is grab a rag and hot water and wash it up. But that process only smears the spot deeper into the carpet. What I now do is simply let the mud dry overnight, then vacuum out the entire spot the next day. Patience is powerful!

The next time you are engulfed by a tidal wave of anger or stress, stop, take a few steps back, and see the situation from a new perspective—God's viewpoint.

I love these words by James Allen: "Tempest-tossed souls, wherever you may be, under whatever conditions you may live, know this: In the ocean of life, the isles of blessedness are smiling, and the sunny shore of your ideal awaits your coming. Self-control is strength. Right thought is mastery. Calmness is power." Allen continues: "The more tranquil a man becomes, the greater is his success, his influence, his power for good. Calmness of mind is one of the beautiful jewels of wisdom."

The waters around you may be raging, yet Jesus is still reaching out His hand, saying, "Peace be still"

(Mark 4:39). Jesus does not have peace; He *is* peace! Whenever we fix our gaze upon Him, peace will flood us automatically.

If you want to experience what it's like to have true power in the midst of all kinds of chaos, learn to *look* to Jesus, then you'll *act* like Jesus.

Remain calm and allow Jesus to channel His serenity through you.

Proverbs 28

1 The wicked run away when no one is chasing them, but the godly are as bold as lions.

2 When there is moral rot within a nation, its government topples easily. But with wise and knowledgeable leaders, there is stability.

3 A poor person who oppresses the poor is like a pounding rain that destroys the crops.

4 To reject the law is to praise the wicked; to obey the law is to fight them.

5 Evil people don't understand justice, but those who follow the Lord understand completely.

6 It is better to be poor and honest than rich and crooked.

7 Young people who obey the law are wise; those who seek out worthless companions bring shame to their parents.

8 A person who makes money by charging interest will lose it. It will end up in the hands of someone who is kind to the poor.

9 The prayers of a person who ignores the law are despised.

10 Those who lead the upright into sin will fall into their own trap, but the honest will inherit good things.

11 Rich people picture themselves as wise, but their real poverty is evident to the poor.

12 When the godly succeed, everyone is glad. When the wicked take charge, people go into hiding.

13 People who cover over their sins will not prosper. But if they confess and forsake them, they will receive mercy.

14 Blessed are those who have a tender conscience, but the stubborn are headed for serious trouble.

15 A wicked ruler is as dangerous to the poor as a lion or bear attacking them.

16 Only a stupid prince will oppress his people, but a king will have a long reign if he hates dishonesty and bribes.

17 A murderer's tormented conscience will drive him into the grave. Don't protect him!

18 The honest will be rescued from harm, but those who are crooked will be destroyed.

19 Hard workers have plenty of food; playing around brings poverty.

20 The trustworthy will get a rich reward. But the person who wants to get rich quick will only get into trouble.

21 Showing partiality is never good, yet some will do wrong for something as small as a piece of bread.

22 A greedy person tries to get rich quick, but it only leads to poverty.

23 In the end, people appreciate frankness more than flattery.

24 Robbing your parents and then saying, "What's wrong with that?" is as serious as committing murder.

25 Greed causes fighting; trusting the Lord leads to prosperity.

26 Trusting oneself is foolish, but those who walk in wisdom are safe.

27 Whoever gives to the poor will lack nothing. But a curse will come upon those who close their eyes to poverty.

28 When the wicked take charge, people hide. When the wicked meet disaster, the godly multiply.

Questions for Reflection:

1. What is the difference between reacting and responding?

2. How do you personally handle tense situations when you're under pressure? What strategies do you use?

3. What part does your spiritual life play in finding peace in times of trouble?

4. Who lately has trampled "mud on your carpet?" Are you exercising patience with that person?

Prayer:

Lord, with the whirlwinds of life all around me, I stand in the quiet center of Your will. Thank You for providing a haven of safety and rest—and for allowing me to experience true peace.

– Secret 29 –
Pursue Your Potential

Be careful of your thoughts;
they may become words at any moment.
– Ira Grassen

Do you consider yourself smart, brilliant, or even a genius? I know you're laughing at this question, and I also know why. You may be thinking that you're *somewhat smart, but brilliant, or a genius? Not a chance!* What if I told you that you *were* a genius? Whether you agree or not, I believe you are! In fact, we all are in certain areas.

James Allen taught that within every acorn there's an oak tree. In every egg, there's a bird.

And inside *us*, there is enormous God-given creative ability, far greater than we can imagine. We only need to trust in God and His plan for our life. I believe that prayer and meditation upon God and His Word causes our creativity to blossom. Why wouldn't it? God created our minds, and we're asking Him, the Creator, how to better use them.

I once heard about a group of Soviet psychologists who researched the capacity and potential of the human mind, and here's what they discovered: A human being's potential is so amazing that if he (or she) used only fifty percent of his mental capacity, he could learn forty languages fluently, memorize the entire encyclopedia from cover to cover, and earn dozens of college and university degrees. It's simply staggering how much potential we human beings possess! And it's all because of the gift of life and a great mind with which God has blessed each of us.

Have you ever wondered why people such as Albert Einstein, Thomas Edison, Walt Disney, Thomas Jefferson, Oprah Winfrey, Bill Gates, Steve Jobs, Steven Spielberg and Al Fike (LOL!) were and are considered to be so brilliant? It's because they have exercised their creative imagination. As Einstein once observed, "Imagination is more important than knowledge."

We all have enormous potential and unmatched creativity. In other words, we are brilliant in our own unique way. God gave each of us the gift of our minds! Sadly, somewhere between the ages of five to seven, most children's creativity seems to get squelched by some parents or relatives, who use such damaging phrases as: "You can't do that" or "Why aren't you smart like your sister?" or "Stop asking so many questions," etc., etc. Unfortunately, a child's imagination and self-confidence can begin the downward spiral from there.

But Solomon didn't take this path. He not only had great knowledge, he also possessed wisdom—because this is what he asked God for! Being smart and brilliant does *not* equate to being wise, because I know some very smart, educated people who do stupid things (like my friend with the firecrackers in Chapter 8). Wisdom can *only* come from God, and it comes *only* when we *ask* for it in faith, with no doubting (see James 1:5-8).

Solomon used this gift of wisdom to lead a nation, serve others and glorify his Creator. For most of his life he was a wise thinker, using his mind for practical matters, as well as thinking about and seeking God.

From the Book of Proverbs, I'd like to share eight characteristics of "Godly thinkers," people whose thinking aligns with and glorifies God:

1. **Godly thinkers are open to the advice of others**. "Fools think they need no advice, but the wise listen to others" (Proverbs 12:15).

2. **Godly thinkers think before speaking.** "There is more hope for a fool than for someone who speaks without thinking" (Proverbs 29:20).

3. **Godly thinkers think before acting.** "Wise people think before they act; fools don't and even brag about it!" (Proverbs 13:16).

4. **Godly thinkers never brag about their insight.** "There is more hope for fools than for people who think they are wise" (Proverbs 26:12).

5. **Godly thinkers play down recognition.** "Just as it is not good to eat too much honey, it is not good for people to think about all the honors they deserve" (Proverbs 25:27).

6. **Godly thinkers understand the proper place of material possessions.** "The rich think of their wealth as an impregnable defense; they imagine it as a high wall of safety" (Proverbs 18:11).

7. **Godly thinkers keep their motives in check.** "People may think they are doing what is right, but the Lord examines the heart" (Proverbs 21:2).

8. **Godly thinkers trust in God, the Originator of right thinking.** "Trust in the Lord with all of your heart and do not lean on your own understanding" (Proverbs 3:5).

We possess the world's most advanced computer, right between our ears! God has given us amazing potential that we habitually fail to use. Do you realize that because much has been granted to us, much is expected in return?

Ask the Lord to open the floodgates of your creativity and correct thinking. Use your mind to think about God every day, and to think of creative ways to advance His Kingdom. Do as the Apostle Paul says: "...have this mind in you which was also in Christ Jesus" (Philippians 2:5).

Don't waste the most valuable gift you possess. Be more creative and use your incredible mind for the glory of God!

Proverbs 29

1 Whoever stubbornly refuses to accept criticism will suddenly be broken beyond repair.

2 When the godly are in authority, the people rejoice. But when the wicked are in power, they groan.

3 The man who loves wisdom brings joy to his father, but if he hangs around with prostitutes, his wealth is wasted.

4 A just king gives stability to his nation, but one who demands bribes destroys it.

5 To flatter people is to lay a trap for their feet.

6 Evil people are trapped by sin, but the righteous escape, shouting for joy.

7 The godly know the rights of the poor; the wicked don't care to know.

8 Mockers can get a whole town agitated, but those who are wise will calm anger.

9 If a wise person takes a fool to court, there will be ranting and ridicule but no satisfaction.

10 The bloodthirsty hate the honest, but the upright seek out the honest.

11 A fool gives full vent to anger, but a wise person quietly holds it back.

12 If a ruler honors liars, all his advisers will be wicked.

13 The poor and the oppressor have this in common— the Lord gives light to the eyes of both.

14 A king who is fair to the poor will have a long reign.

15 To discipline and reprimand a child produces wisdom, but a mother is disgraced by an undisciplined child.

16 When the wicked are in authority, sin increases. But the godly will live to see the tyrant's downfall.

17 Discipline your children, and they will give you happiness and peace of mind.

18 When people do not accept divine guidance, they run wild. But whoever obeys the law is happy.

19 For a servant, mere words are not enough— discipline is needed. For the words may be understood, but they are not heeded.

20 There is more hope for a fool than for someone who speaks without thinking.

21 A servant who is pampered from childhood will later become a rebel.

22 A hot-tempered person starts fights and gets into all kinds of sin.

23 Pride ends in humiliation, while humility brings honor.

24 If you assist a thief, you are only hurting yourself. You will be punished if you report the crime, but you will be cursed if you don't.

25 Fearing people is a dangerous trap, but to trust the Lord means safety.

26 Many seek the ruler's favor, but justice comes from the Lord.

27 The godly despise the wicked; the wicked despise the godly.

Questions for Reflection:

1. Do your current goals inspire you to exercise your creativity?

2. How much time do you spend each day thinking about God's promises and plans for your life? How can that time be expanded? (For example: Cutting back on TV, etc.)

3. What is the Lord calling you to do that might require more focused thought and planning?

4. How much do you think about the Lord Himself, for Who He is, and not simply what He can do for you?

Prayer:

Father, You are the giver of every perfect gift. Please fill my thoughts with creativity far beyond my own ability. I will give You the praise and thanks for fulfilling Your promise in me. Thank you for my incredible mind!

– Secret 30 –
Be a Blessing

God particularly pours out His blessings upon those who know how much they need Him.
– Robert H. Schuller

Back in 1979 and 1980, I was leading several summer youth camps at a Christian Conference Center in New Mexico.

On Father's Day, 1979, during some afternoon free time, I wrote my Dad a "thank you" letter. I poured out my heart to him and, for the first time, thanked him for—as much as I could remember—all he had done for us three kids: teaching us about the Lord, taking us to church, even buying me a battery-operated toy helicopter for no particular reason. I went on and on.

My mother later shared with me what that letter meant to him. "Big tears came to his eyes," she said. Since my father had blessed me in so many ways, I wanted to return the blessing by thanking Him. My parents went far beyond measure in helping us three children at various times in our lives. They gave sacrificially, and have always been a blessing to us.

Dad and Mom have since gone on to be with the Lord, and we miss them very much. They blessed us with good gifts, even when we didn't know what we needed, or what to ask for. Even as Christians, we sometimes don't know what to ask the Lord for, but He blesses us anyway. I love that about Him!

For the past 30 lessons and chapters of Proverbs, you've been reading about the blessing of wisdom God gave Solomon. But where did this outpouring of divine understanding begin?

Let's look back at Solomon, this son of King David, as he was about to become the leader of Israel. God appeared to him and said, "What do you want? Ask, and I will give it to you!" (2 Chronicles 1:7).

Solomon replied, "...you have made me king over a people as numerous as the dust of the earth! Give me wisdom and knowledge to rule them properly, for who is able to govern this great nation of yours?" (vv.9-10).

The Lord answered, "Because your greatest desire is to help your people, and you did not ask for personal wealth and honor or the death of your enemies or even a long life, but rather you asked for wisdom and knowledge to properly govern my people, I will certainly give you the wisdom and knowledge you requested" (vv.11-12). Then God promised Solomon what he did *not* request: "And I will also give you riches, wealth, and honor such as no other king has ever had before you or will ever have again!" (v.12).

What a gift! The richest man who ever lived received God's greatest blessings as a by-product of having a pure heart at this time in his life. He wanted God and His wisdom above anything else. What a pure prayer to offer God!

This verse serves as a great model: "...give me neither poverty nor riches! Give me just enough to satisfy my needs" (Proverbs 30:8).

When the Lord hears such a sincere, humble request, He can't wait to open the windows of heaven.

I hope you'll think for a moment just how fortunate and blessed we truly are. These are a few of the things I'm personally grateful for (in no particular order):

- I am blessed to live in this great country.
- I am blessed to have God's unconditional love.
- I am blessed with the Bible to show me how to live.

- I am blessed by having Jesus Christ become the sacrifice and substitute for my sin.
- I am blessed with a great family.
- I am blessed with gifts, talents and the ability to work.
- I am blessed with a wonderful mind.
- I am blessed with the capacity to dream, hope and achieve wonderful things for the Lord.
- I am blessed with eyes to see and ears to hear.
- Most of all, I am blessed with the gift of eternal life *right now* and not just later! This life began for me at the age of nine—the moment I put my faith and trust in God through Jesus Christ.

It's really true that, "The godly are showered with blessings" (Proverbs 10:6). Our Heavenly Father is so good to us and blesses us with so much. How can we not live a life that pleases Him as a way to "thank you?"

I hope you'll make it your ambition to allow God to bless others through you, and to share the Good News that God loves them and wants to have a personal relationship with them. What greater gift is there that this?

Now, everywhere you go, bring that blessing with you to share with others.

Proverbs 30

1 The message of Agur son of Jakeh. An oracle. I am weary, O God; I am weary and worn out, O God.

2 I am too ignorant to be human, and I lack common sense.

3 I have not mastered human wisdom, nor do I know the Holy One.

4 Who but God goes up to heaven and comes back down? Who holds the wind in his fists? Who wraps up the oceans in his cloak? Who has created the whole wide world? What is his name – and his son's name? Tell me if you know!

5 Every word of God proves true. He defends all who come to him for protection.

6 Do not add to his words, or he may rebuke you, and you will be found a liar.

7 O God, I beg two favors from you before I die.

8 First, help me never to tell a lie. Second, give me neither poverty nor riches! Give me just enough to satisfy my needs.

9 For if I grow rich, I may deny you and say, "Who is the Lord?" And if I am too poor, I may steal and thus insult God's holy name.

10 Never slander a person to his employer. If you do, the person will curse you, and you will pay for it.

11 Some people curse their father and do not thank their mother.

12 They feel pure, but they are filthy and unwashed.

13 They are proud beyond description and disdainful.

14 They devour the poor with teeth as sharp as swords or knives. They destroy the needy from the face of the earth.

15 The leech has two suckers that cry out, "More, more!" There are three other things—no, four!—that are never satisfied:

16 the grave, the barren womb, the thirsty desert, the blazing fire.

17 The eye that mocks a father and despises a mother will be plucked out by ravens of the valley and eaten by vultures.

18 There are three things that amaze me—no, four things I do not understand:

19 how an eagle glides through the sky, how a snake slithers on a rock, how a ship navigates the ocean, how a man loves a woman.

20 Equally amazing is how an adulterous woman can satisfy her sexual appetite, shrug her shoulders, and then say, "What's wrong with that?"

21 There are three things that make the earth tremble—no, four it cannot endure:

22 a slave who becomes a king, an overbearing fool who prospers,

23 a bitter woman who finally gets a husband, a servant girl who supplants her mistress.

24 There are four things on earth that are small but unusually wise:

25 Ants—they aren't strong, but they store up food for the winter.

26 Rock badgers—they aren't powerful, but they make their homes among the rocky cliffs.

27 Locusts—they have no king, but they march like an army in ranks.

28 Lizards—they are easy to catch, but they are found even in kings' palaces.

29 There are three stately monarchs on the earth— no, four:

30 the lion, king of animals, who won't turn aside for anything,

31 the strutting rooster, the male goat, a king as he leads his army.

32 If you have been a fool by being proud or plotting evil, don't brag about it—cover your mouth with your hand in shame.

33 As the beating of cream yields butter, and a blow to the nose causes bleeding, so anger causes quarrels.

Questions for Reflection:

1. Name a minimum of ten things for which you are grateful to God.

2. Have you taken the time to thank those who have enriched your life? Would you send them an email, or a hand-written note (which is much better)?

3. How do you express your gratitude to the Lord for His goodness using your words? What about in your actions?

Prayer:

Father, I praise You for granting me blessings far more than I deserve. Your provision in my life is abundant. Most of all, thank You for sending Your Son, Jesus, who gave Himself so that I could have eternal life.

– Secret 31 –
Value the Valuable

What sir, would the people of the earth be without
woman? They would be scarce, sir, mighty scarce.
–Mark Twain

All-righty then, let's cut to the chase. When God created woman, it was an awesome idea!

Without women, men are pretty much useless. My wife has had jobs with a few different companies over the years. As an Executive Assistant, her job is to make the boss look great—and she's an expert at it! There are bosses I know personally that, if they didn't have a great female assistant behind them, I'm telling you, they'd be fired in less than a week! Might I add in defense of the female gender, most women make better bosses than men because they use their brains better than we do. We men are just dumb and stupid sometimes (my wife loves to hear me say this). We need help big time! Thus, God created woman!

God has used—and continues to use—women to accomplish great things for the Kingdom.

One person who prominently comes to my mind is Mary. She was chosen by God as the instrument to bring Christ, the Savior, into the world. And just look at her journey. She was with Jesus, not just in His beginning, adolescent, and early adult years, but she followed Him all the way to the crucifixion—His death! And get a load of this: as Christ was being led away to die, every one of the disciples (men, mind you) fled the scene except for John. But Mary (and the other women) followed and stayed with Jesus all the way to watch Him hang on a cross for our sins! Talk about courage!

When I think of all the women in my life, I'm extremely grateful. My maternal grandmother was so gracious and loving. My mom was awesome! She worked hard all her life and always made our family a top priority. She was a wonderful mother!

My sister, Pam, is not only a great sibling, but a wonderful friend. She was there with me during some of the darkest days of my life. There's nothing like an understanding sister!

Katie, my beautiful daughter, has always been the apple of my eye. God has used her to teach me patience (especially during her teenage years!) She is a caring mother toward our grandsons and a loving wife to Logan. I can see it in her eyes; she would sacrifice anything for their well-being.

Natalie, who belongs to my first wife, Vicki and Wayne (my "husband-in-law" LOL!) is just a special gift from heaven for all of us.

Then there's my wife, Carolyn. She is the best thing that ever happened to me! Today's chapter describes exactly how I feel about her: "There are many virtuous and capable women in the world, but you surpass them all" (Proverbs 31:29).

Carolyn has always been a great support. She works hard and takes great pride in our home. She is also an excellent cook, as I mentioned earlier (she's written a cookbook and has another one on the way). Cooking is her gift and skill that she uses to bless others who are going through difficult times. Nothing speaks like food, right? She truly lives out the Proverb, "She extends a helping hand" (v.20).

Proverbs concludes with a portrait of a woman of strong character, great wisdom, many skills, and heartfelt compassion. She is an excellent wife and mother—and a very hard worker. Her strength and dignity are the result of her reverence for God.

Although her appearance is never mentioned, her attractiveness flows from her character, which is her solid foundation. She serves as a role model of integrity and resourcefulness for all women—whether married or single.

Here are two unique traits to be appreciated in women:

1. Intuition—A woman's radar can pick up on stuff a man will never get—he doesn't even know what a radar is! But she has "feelings" and "hunches" about people or situations that are usually right on target. When our wives say, "I just don't feel quite right about this," we men better stop, take a deep breath, and wait a while before moving forward on that "business deal." Bankruptcy could be around the corner. After living with such a woman, I try to pay better attention to her signals. Here's an example of how they pick up on things: You're lying in bed at 2:00 A.M. when your wife suddenly punches you, while you're still in a coma, and says, "Something's wrong—go check." Of course, you know that "nothing is wrong." So, you reluctantly get up anyway just to appease her, and discover the garage door is wide open! *Amazing! How do they know that stuff?* God has blessed them with incredible insight and intuition!

2. Tenacity—If you mess with baby cubs, it's not the daddy bear you'll have to answer to—it's the Mama! She'll have you for lunch! Men sometimes think women are the "weaker" sex, but just watch what happens when the upright piano falls over on one of the kids, or the pet. Women have a reserve tank of strength that is seldom seen until needed. Never, ever, underestimate their power and determination, especially in dire circumstances!

I can't think of a better way to close this chapter than with these words: "Charm is deceptive, and beauty does not last; but a woman who fears the Lord will be greatly praised" (v.30).

Where would we be—*what* would we be—without the valuable treasure of a godly woman?

Proverbs 31

1 These are the sayings of King Lemuel, an oracle that his mother taught him.

2 O my son, O son of my womb, O son of my promises,

3 do not spend your strength on women, on those who ruin kings.

4 And it is not for kings, O Lemuel, to guzzle wine. Rulers should not crave liquor.

5 For if they drink, they may forget their duties and be unable to give justice to those who are oppressed.

6 Liquor is for the dying, and wine for those in deep depression.

7 Let them drink to forget their poverty and remember their troubles no more.

8 Speak up for those who cannot speak for themselves; ensure justice for those who are perishing.

9 Yes, speak up for the poor and helpless, and see that they get justice.

A Wife of Noble Character

10 Who can find a virtuous and capable wife? She is worth more than precious rubies.

11 Her husband can trust her, and she will greatly enrich his life.

12 She will not hinder him but help him all her life.

13 She finds wool and flax and busily spins it.

14 She is like a merchant's ship; she brings her food from afar.

15 She gets up before dawn to prepare breakfast for her household and plan the day's work for her servant girls.

16 She goes out to inspect a field and buys it; with her earnings she plants a vineyard.

17 She is energetic and strong, a hard worker.

18 She watches for bargains; her lights burn late into the night.

19 Her hands are busy spinning thread, her fingers twisting fiber.

20 She extends a helping hand to the poor and opens her arms to the needy.

21 She has no fear of winter for her household because all of them have warm clothes.

22 She quilts her own bedspreads. She dresses like royalty in gowns of finest cloth.

23 Her husband is well known, for he sits in the council meeting with the other civic leaders.

24 She makes belted linen garments and sashes to sell to the merchants.

25 She is clothed with strength and dignity, and she laughs with no fear of the future.

26 When she speaks, her words are wise, and kindness is the rule when she gives instructions.

27 She carefully watches all that goes on in her household and does not have to bear the consequences of laziness.

28 Her children stand and bless her. Her husband praises her:

29 "There are many virtuous and capable women in the world, but you surpass them all!"

30 Charm is deceptive, and beauty does not last; but a woman who fears the Lord will be greatly praised.

31 Reward her for all she has done. Let her deeds publicly declare her praise.

Questions for Reflection:

1. Regardless of gender, how does your character measure up to the "Proverbs 31" woman?
2. What can you do to show heart-felt appreciation to your spouse?
3. What do you tend to notice first in others—appearance or character?

Prayer:

Lord, You have wonderfully made man and woman. We are different, and that's a good thing. This allows us to complement each other. Teach us to never take each other for granted, because we certainly need each other. Help us both as a couple and believers to individually seek YOU first; and as a result, we will automatically be drawn closer to each other.

Conclusion

As you complete this 31-success journey, it is my prayer that you will apply God's wisdom to your every thought and action. Once you view life—and how to live—from His perspective, it'll begin to make sense.

If you're already a follower of Christ, spend time with Him each day by praying to Him and reading in His love letter—the Bible.

If you have never trusted Christ as your Lord and Savior, here are some verses I'd like to share with you to guide you in making the most important decision of your life. I like to call these verses the "six numbers to the combination lock of eternal life." They are found in the wonderful book of Romans by the Apostle Paul:

Combination # 1- (3:23)
Admit that you have sinned against God.

Romans 3:23 says, "For all have sinned and fall short of the glory of God."

Combination # 2- (6:23)
Realize there's a payment for breaking God's law.

Romans 6:23 says, "For the wages of sin is death, but the gift of God is eternal life."

Combination # 3- (5:8)
Understand that He loves you and has provided a way out from the penalty of your sin (violation) through Christ.

Romans 5:8 says, "But God showed His love toward us, in that while we yet sinners, Christ died for us."

Combination # 4- (10:9)
Confess that Jesus is the Lord and believe that He is alive.

Romans 10:9 says, "That if you confess with your mouth the Lord Jesus, and believe in your heart that God raised him from the dead, you shall be saved."

Combination # 5- (10:13)
Call upon Him to forgive your sins and to save you.

Romans 10:13 says, "Whosoever shall call upon the name of the Lord shall be saved."

Combination # 6- (3:16)
Accept His offer—the free gift of eternal life.

John 3:16 says, "For God so loved the world, He gave His only begotten son, that whosoever believes in Him, should not perish, but have eternal life."

Salvation is a gift—it's FREE—already paid for by Jesus' blood and sacrificial death on the cross. You CANNOT earn His grace; you can only ACCEPT it (see Ephesians 2:8-9)

Follow the numbers in the sequence, and the "combination lock" of eternal life opens. What are you waiting for? The Lord's loving arms are wide open, waiting for you to come....PLEASE TRUST HIM NOW!

Acknowledgments

I am very thankful for:

- My incredible wife, Carolyn—I could not have written this book without her. She means the world to me and she is my true love and helpmate.
- My awesome children and grandkids.

I am also deeply grateful to my many friends who've been such an inspiration and encouragement to me:

- The Heights Baptist Church, Richardson, TX (where I teach a Bible study)
- Bubba and Cindy Cathy and their wonderful business, Chick-fil-A
- Jim and Lisa Meyerhoff, Matt and Donna Howell, and Robert and Jane Hanna
- David Alvey, for proofing and editing, and being a super friend.
- Melissa Nader for proofing and editing

But I must thank *you*, my reader friends, for reading and sharing this book (e-book). As I said earlier, I pretty much wrote this book for myself; then I thought *if it helped me, hopefully it would encourage others.* I hope this is the case.

I'm truly blessed to have so many brothers and sisters in Christ around the world. I haven't met most of you, but we will one day meet in heaven!

Thank you all so much!

-Al Fike

Contact Information

FOR A COMPLETE LIST OF PRODUCTS BY AL FIKE,
OR TO SCHEDULE AL FOR A SPEAKING OR COMEDY
ENGAGEMENT, CONTACT:

AL FIKE
201 West Renner Rd (THBC)
Richardson, Texas 75080
Booking: 214-766-0969
Web: www.alfike.com
Email: alfike@alfike.com
YouTube: www.youtube.com/alfike
Facebook: www.facebook.com/aljfike
Twitter: www.twitter.com/alfike (@alfike)
Al's blog: http://alfike.blogspot.com
Linked In: http://www.linkedin.com/in/alfike

**Copies of this book (paperback and digital) can be
ordered on: Amazon.com and CreateSpace.com**

Audio CDs and MP3s are available at alfike.com.

About Al Fike

Al Fike is an inspirational speaker, teacher, leadership trainer, minister and noted Christian Comedian. He has been called "One of the most entertaining and motivating speakers in the country today." Bob Hope called Al "a real nut!"

Al has been featured on the Fox News Channel, Trinity Broadcasting Network, ABC, and has made many other national TV and radio appearances.

But he's much more than just an entertainer. He's passionate about pointing others to Jesus Christ and encouraging believers to walk closer with God.

He's also wants to help YOU achieve your God-given potential by absorbing the secrets of success from a true Wise Guy, King Solomon, the author of the greatest book of wisdom ever written—the Book of Proverbs.

Al is a graduate of William Carey University in Hattiesburg, Mississippi, and earned his Master of Divinity degree from New Orleans Baptist Theological Seminary.

He has 3 grown children and 5 grandkids. He and his wife, Carolyn, live in the Dallas, Texas area.

You can find out more at: www.alfike.com, as well as Facebook (aljfike) and Twitter (@alfike).

Notes:

Notes:

Notes:

Made in the USA
Columbia, SC
11 September 2019